"Asthma is striking for the confusion it causes in the medical profession, and Brookes is a gifted investigator with just the right amount of skepticism."   —*The New Yorker*

"You ought to caution readers not to open this book if they have something important to do in the next few hours. Whatever it was will not get done until they've taken the whole trip. It's a grabber."   —Daniel Pinkwater

"It is authenticity that makes *Catching My Breath* compelling reading. Ultimately it is a rallying cry for asthmatics. . . . Tim Brookes speaks [their] language."   —*Cleveland Plain Dealer*

"Gripping. . . . With a deft talent for crafting urgent prose, Brookes describes 'the real thing.' *Catching My Breath* is a medical detective story with attitude, part science textbook, part sociological study, part health-care polemic and, ultimately, a how-to on redefining what it means to be ill."
     —*Vermont Times*

"An unconventional exploration of illness [and] a hard look at the mysteries of asthma."   —*Milwaukee Journal*

"*Catching My Breath* is a literate investigation of asthma from just about every conceivable angle. Brookes is a journalist who knows how to research a subject. Strong reporting, nicely balanced between the subjective and the objective."
     —*Kirkus Reviews*

TIM BROOKES'S

Catching My Breath

Tim Brookes was born and brought up in England and has lived in the United States since 1980. He has worked as a writer, a musician, a teacher, a soccer coach, an editor, and a film reviewer, and currently he teaches at the University of Vermont. Mr. Brookes is also a regular essayist for National Public Radio's Sunday *Weekend Edition* and a journalist whose work has appeared in *The New York Times Magazine*, *The Atlantic*, and *The Boston Globe*. He now regards himself as a recovering asthmatic.

TIM BROOKES

Catching My Breath

An Asthmatic Explores

His Illness

VINTAGE BOOKS

A Division of Random House, Inc. New York

To Margaret, Barbara, and Zoë

FIRST VINTAGE BOOKS EDITION, JUNE 1995

Copyright © 1994, 1995 by Tim Brookes

All rights reserved under International and Pan-American Copyright
Conventions. Published in the United States by Vintage Books,
a division of Random House, Inc., New York, and simultaneously in
Canada by Random House of Canada Limited, Toronto.
Originally published in hardcover by Times Books, a division
of Random House, Inc., New York, in 1994.

The Library of Congress has cataloged the Times Books
edition as follows:

Brookes, Tim.
Catching my breath: an asthmatic explores his illness/Tim Brookes.—
1st ed.
p. cm.
ISBN 0-8129-2182-8
1. Asthma. I. Title.
RC591.B765 1994
616.2'38—dc20 93-44737
Vintage ISBN: 0-679-76206-X

Design by Naomi Osnos and M. Kristen Bearse

Manufactured in the United States of America

10 9 8 7 6 5 4 3 2 1

Acknowledgments

I would never have thought of writing this book had it not been for the kindness and generosity of Bill Jasperson, who called me as a complete stranger and said, "You should be writing books," and recommended me to his agent, Henry Dunow.

Even though I approached them as an amateur and one who was not always in agreement with received medical wisdom, virtually everyone in the medical profession I spoke to was courteous and encouraging. Dave Babbott, Art Bergner, Ann Bunting, Stan Burns, Mike Charlton, John Clarke, Larry Coffin, Nils Deaulaire, Barbara Frankowski, Howard Frumkin, Dave Gannon, Tom Gazda, Ed Golub, John Heisse, Eileen Humphrey, Joseph Jarvis, Harvey Klein, Bryan Lask, Kevin Leslie, Charlie McLean, Bill Mercia, John Pietropaoli, Dennis Plante, Thomas Platts-Mills, Sandy Reider, Alan Rubin, Nancy Rubin, Roger Secker-Walker, Gerry Silverstein, Steve Sirch, Ray Slavin, Don Swartz, David Tormey, Howard Waitzkin, and Brad Weiss were especially helpful and informative.

I'd also like to thank the staffs of the New York Children's Health Project and the Dana Medical Library at the

University of Vermont; Colin Harrison and Louise Piche, who gave good advice of wildly varying kinds: Pamela Walters and Jeff Lawton, who helped with fact-checking; and Arthur Fiacco, Marilyn Grigas, Terry Ranney, Jillie and Sophie Gazda, Alison James, and all the other asthmatics and parents of asthmatics who've told me their histories, their symptoms, and their beliefs. Also three mentors: David Huddle, who always encouraged me to write, even when I thought I was a novelist; Josh Mamis, who first gave me the opportunity to write journalism with a personal voice, even if he could pay only twenty dollars an article; and Louise Glück, who unwittingly convinced me that I was not a poet.

The book could probably not have been written without the support of Jim and Donna Carlson at the Swedish Pit, who twice fixed my car even though they knew I couldn't pay them.

In addition to giving me a great deal of their time and advice, Ed Kent, Larry Coffin, Bob Klein, Tom Gazda, Bryan Lask, and Tim Thompson were kind enough to proof the manuscript for errors and to make helpful suggestions of their own. Anything I failed to understand or refused to listen to is not their fault.

Finally, to my cheerful and encouraging editor at Times Books, Betsy Rapoport, and her family, many thanks and best wishes.

Contents

Catching My Breath

"Who is suffering? The asthmatic or his environment? And what precisely is the nature of his suffering?"

—AARON LASK, *Asthma: Attitude and Milieu*

Prologue

A t half past midnight, my stomach suddenly felt uneasy. This was hardly unusual: for the past month, barely a day had gone by without heartburn. I sat up in bed and groped for the Rolaids. By the time I found them my stomach was acidic, turbulent. I ate two. Within a few minutes my entire metabolism changed. My sinuses were swelling, stiffening, filling up, my ears and cheeks getting hot, my spine and my chin itching. Everything was closing in around my throat and chest; I felt a frightening internal claustrophobia, a sense of metabolic urgency rapidly mounting toward panic.

I already knew this was no ordinary asthma attack. I had had my first attack nearly thirty years ago, and despite desensitizing injections, preventive medications, steroid shots, psychotherapy, and even a course of injections of tobacco leaf, silver, and blackthorn, prescribed by a homeopath and administered gingerly by my girlfriend, I didn't grow out of it, as the doctors had said I might. Over the years, I came to recognize several kinds of asthma: most were a lighter or heavier wheeze that came on gradually late in the evening, or more suddenly when shoveling snow in a heavy coat. These attacks sounded like the word *asthma,* a sibilant rasp. Three times since I'd turned thirty, though, something entirely different had happened, a sudden, overwhelming assault that stormed through my whole body, seizing my throat and suffocating me. This felt like one of those asthmas.

I swung my legs over the side of the bed and put my palms on my knees in the classic asthma breathing position, wondering what the hell had brought this attack on. It felt as if I'd eaten something I was allergic to, what with the reaction throughout my whole body, the weird stomach. But what had I eaten? Fontina cheese and crackers; a bottle of Dos Equis and a bottle of Grolsch; pumpkin pie and ice cream—nothing I hadn't had before. Rolaids? I'd been taking them for a decade. Weren't they just chalk?

Well, what about stress? Christ, what stress wasn't I under? I was going through a divorce, I was teaching four classes at the university on top of my usual freelance writing—but could stress really cause an attack this bad?

I fumbled around on my night table and found a Primatene inhaler, the kind you used to see advertised on television with Jackie Joyner-Kersee taking a quick hit, recovering in fifteen seconds, and then sprinting to a gold medal. It's an over-the-counter medication some doctors view askance, knowing its potential for unfortunate cardiac side effects. But my prescribed albuterol inhaler didn't seem to help much anymore; I suspected I was becoming allergic to the propellant—a disturbing thought. The Primatene seemed to work better, so my GP had shrugged and said, "Sure. Give it a try." I squeezed the Primatene and drew the spray in deeply.

For a few seconds I thought it had worked. But even as

I breathed a little more easily, I felt the mounting urgency of the attack in the rest of my system: my sinuses were now completely solid and swelling further, pressing against my cheeks and eyes. My face, ears, and neck were burning, and a desperate itch was running up and down my spine.

I had to get to some epinephrine. Also known as adrenaline, it was what I had been given when I had been rushed to the hospital with my first asthma emergency; since then I had been trained to inject myself in the thigh and carried an Ana-Kit, short for anaphylaxis kit, around with me. Once, during a moderately severe attack, I had decided to give myself a half-dose, just for practice, and it had worked fine: easy to inject, swift relief.

I woke Barbara, my girlfriend. She had never seen a major asthma attack before; I knew that it would probably be more frightening for her than for me. From the outside, the sufferer of asthmatic anaphylaxis looks as if he is collapsing inward, drowning in an invisible sea of himself. "In the car," I said, trying to show calm, measuring my phrases to fit the amount of air that I could muster. "In the glove compartment. Is my epinephrine syringe. Please go and get it. Right away. Here are the keys."

Alarmed, she dressed hurriedly and ran out.

The attack was accelerating. By now I had two hearts, one in each ear. The effects of the Primatene had been overrun, and I felt my chest and throat tightening around my windpipe. My upper body had *become* panic, operating with a life and purpose of its own. I felt as if my intelligence had been suddenly separated from a body gone amok, and left alone and in charge, like the captain of a torpedoed ship with six deckloads of passengers and crew milling around and beneath him, screaming, and the engines driving the ship straight down. But the epinephrine would stop all this. Everything would be all right as soon as the epinephrine arrived.

Barbara burst in with the kit, not the half-used Ana-Kit but an ostensibly more sophisticated tool I had been given since, an EpiPen syringe, commonly prescribed for those with potentially fatal bee-sting allergies. When I opened the tube, I saw that to my surprise it didn't look like a syringe but a large grey ballpoint without a nib. *Press against thigh and hold in place for ten seconds.* I did so. Nothing happened. I pressed my thumb against the butt-end; perhaps I had to push the needle in myself. Still nothing. How did this damn thing work? I jabbed it harder against my leg, there was a thudding noise, and I felt the needle ram into my muscle with not a stabbing pain but that deep, unnerving thump that is the real sensation of a stab wound. I was startled—but at least the epinephrine was going in. Now things would be all right.

To be on the safe side, I waited thirty seconds before withdrawing the needle. As it came out, I was surprised first at the length of it—no wonder they keep it retracted—and then at the sudden rush of blood. *This shouldn't be happening!* I cupped my hand under it, yelling for a paper towel. Three fat drops seeped between my fingers and spread into the white cotton rug. Next morning they would be the only visible signs of the night's events.

Within a couple of minutes it became clear that the epinephrine wasn't working. Had it all bled out? Had I developed a resistance to it? What the hell was going on?

Asthma feeds on panic; asthma *is* panic. I breathed from my diaphragm, the way they teach you as a child, and calculated. The Primatene, unlike the albuterol inhalers, contains epinephrine—0.3 mg per dose, I thought. I had just injected myself with another 1 mg. How much would it take? What would happen if I took too much?

This is the paradox of chronic illness: the patient grows around the disease, like an oak tree engulfing a barbed-wire fence. My own habits and shortcomings probably perpetuate the condition; the asthma disappears under the bark of my character where I am least likely to look for it. The answer, it would seem, is to remain vigilant, to inform oneself of the latest research, the newest medicines—but such vigilance shades into hypochondria; and, more importantly, anxiety brings on asthma. Research suggests that those who worry most about asthma are probably those who resort more swiftly to the inhaler; and there's nothing so terrible as the sight of someone sucking on an inhaler every half hour, a slave to her own salvation. *Breathe slowly,* I told myself; *think quickly.*

It was an eerie, vertiginous feeling: I was confronting the normally unexamined mechanics of staying alive, like the clock face turning and staring at the movement in its own case. What are the most vital functions? Breathing. Heartbeat. Brain activity. Of these only breathing is at all voluntary. The cardiac patient, sensing the onset of arrest, can't will his heart back to its measured beat, soothing it down from a frightening erratic fibrillation; he can't rip open his chest and squeeze once a second, his life literally in his own hands. Only with breathing are we given the devil's option, the chance to keep ourselves going by force of will.

Barbara was trying to stroke my neck, asking questions. My irritation rose like the flush in my skin. "In the kitchen," I told her. "Opposite the sink. Top shelf. Ana-Kit. Orange plastic box. Rectangular. Under the sink. Bottle of alcohol. Get them both *now*."

She found the half-used Ana-Kit and the alcohol. *I've used the needle before, so it will have to be sterilized,* reasoned my intelligence, pacing the bridge, though I had no idea whether dipping the needle in alcohol would kill all the germs, nor whether at this stage that even mattered. I dabbled it briefly, then jabbed it at my thigh. It bounced off. Maybe the needle had been blunted, and wouldn't work a second time? I pushed harder and it drove through the skin as if through linoleum. I gave myself another 0.5 mg of epinephrine. This, surely, would be enough.

I sat on the edge of the bed, naked, hauling in breath, bent over like a coalman hauling his sack. The epinephrine did not work.

I used to live near Accles & Pollock, in Worcestershire, the company that according to *The Guinness Book of Records* made the thinnest tubing in the world at the time, its bore being a thousandth of an inch, or something like that, more a thread than a tube. That's what my trachea felt like. *I can get just enough air to survive if I don't move or talk, if I can focus on the muscles in my throat and convince them not to contract still further.* Even so, I realized I was better off than during my first major attack, in 1984, when that thread of a tube filled up with fluid and I knew what it is like to drown.

I was dimly aware that Barbara was asking, "Shall I call an ambulance?" I nodded. My face felt stretched, like Edvard Munch's screamer, but silent. I thought of an elderly woman I once knew who had died slowly, losing touch with her surroundings, sinking in on herself, confused, muffled, protected from knowing what was happening as if the body had released some hormone that made it all not matter very much. *That's how I want to die,* I thought. *Anything but dying fully aware and in a panic.*

My head had started aching. By now sharp pains shot through my back whenever I breathed in. Technically, asthma is caused by not being able to breathe *out*; people have died with substantial amounts of air trapped in their lungs. It doesn't feel that way to an asthmatic: breathing in is inspiration, clutching for the straw of air. Breathing in is the beginning of life, the first gulp as the diver reaches the surface. No asthmatic works to breathe out.

The fire crew arrived and flitted around like shadows—dark, unimportant, almost unreal. I've read that to an addict, nothing but his drug matters; and at this point I knew that this must be true in a literal sense: *Nothing but the drug has matter.* Everything outside me was insubstantial, at most only a distraction, an irritation. Shades of people moved around the room, asking questions I couldn't answer, murmuring to each other, their walkie-talkies crackling. The only person I wanted to see was the one with the cure, which would give him or her definition and meaning. Sartre was wrong: we are given not only meaning but existence by our acts. Barbara and the fire crew couldn't help, so they vanished; I shrank further into myself and worked on giving myself existence by breathing.

At one point the panic rose like a wave and engulfed me. "Help me," I croaked to one of the fire crew. He stared at me. *He doesn't know what to do,* I thought. *I shouldn't have involved him.* I turned back into the internal world, where I was needed and could be of some use.

The ambulance crew arrived. "Do you feel as if you're going to pass out?" they asked. I worked up enough air to talk. "I feel. As if. I'm going to die." That answer didn't fit their criteria for an informative response, and at once it became clear that they couldn't do anything to help me either, but at least we would be off to the emergency room, which was only a few minutes up the hill. First, though, they had to get me out of the house. "Can you put your clothes on? Can you get into the chair?" they asked, and when I didn't answer they thought I was being stubborn, or I couldn't understand them. They repeated the questions several times, but in the sick man's solipsistic wisdom I knew better than they: the slightest movement, even talking, involved constricting some group of muscles, and every muscle was now connected to my chest, pressing on it. I had to plan every movement ahead, to imagine the most efficient, the most graceful way of doing it, then wait half a minute to relax as best I could, make the movement, and collapse into myself afterward as my pulse shot up and my hearts pounded in my ears, my thread of air temporarily crushed. I felt like a dwarf—large head, barrel chest, puny arms, virtually nonexistent below the diaphragm. I had shrunk to all that mattered. It amazed me that when I finally half-stood I was taller than they.

Once in the ambulance, breathing oxygen through a mask, I knew the worst was over. Relatively few people die of asthma once they get to the hospital, though I was still alarmed that the epinephrine hadn't worked. In the ER, the doctors and nurses asked me, "Can you tell us what's wrong?" Astonished and angry that they couldn't see that I couldn't speak, I grabbed the pen from someone's breast pocket and wrote on the paper sheet on the examining table what had happened, and how much epinephrine I had already taken. They changed my oxygen mask for an albuterol one and within minutes my breathing began to clear—a strange sensation, like someone removing thick cobwebs one by one—and I began to notice my headache and nausea. "That'll be from the epinephrine," the nurse said, though she had no idea why, if I had so much of the drug in my system, the attack had ridden roughshod over it. She brought me a bowl, into which I threw up, and acetaminophen suppositories, which I accepted with the lack of dignity of one to whom other people barely exist.

I sat on the table for an hour and a half, unwinding, my muscles unwrapping themselves until I was no longer a clenched triangle but could sit back against the pillow as the external world returned. I felt as if I had been inside out. The staff was as surprised that a major attack had passed so quickly as they were baffled as to what had caused it. Within two hours I was shaky, but breathing normally; at 4 A.M. I shuffled out to the lobby in lime-green hospital slippers and took a taxi home.

In the emergency room, as the attack eased away, I wondered if afterward I would have that transformative experience of seeing the world afresh in all the glory that I had been overlooking; then, when that seemed unlikely, I wondered if I would emerge like Coleridge's wedding-guest, a sadder but wiser man. In fact, I was no wiser at all, as far as I could tell. Instead, it felt as if I had been visited during the night by a bear that had filled the room with a blacker darkness for a terrifying long moment and then lumbered out, leaving me wondering how the hell it had got in and whether it could return, and leaving also a faint but perfectly distinct odor that might be the creature or might be my own smell of panic.

Over the next month, five doctors in five different fields of medicine proposed five different theories as to what had caused my attack, and even disagreed over whether it should be called asthma or anaphylaxis, a dangerous, widespread allergic reaction that causes different symptoms—itching, hives, sneezing, heavy production of mucus, diarrhea, asthma—in different people. A common feature is that tissues swell considerably; if the airway tissues swell too much, the sufferer can choke to death. The leading local allergist had me tested for allergies—excluding Fontina, beer, and Rolaids, but including gerbils, as I admitted that four months previously I had bought my daughter a gerbil. The tests showed that I was still allergic to the same grasses, pollens, and molds that I had reacted to in 1965 after my first attack. The gerbil, however, was blameless.

The allergist prescribed a preventive approach: a different inhaler, which propelled corticosteroids into my lungs—not anabolic steroids, he reassured me: I was in no danger of compiling immense muscle mass or acquir-

ing unfashionable secondary sexual characteristics. Corticosteroids suppress inflammation, he said, at which I nodded as though I should understand. He refused to
speculate on what might have caused the attack, or
whether epinephrine would work next time, or whether
the inhaled steroids offered any chance of long-term improvement. I left feeling as if I were on my own.

How would asthma limit my life? Would I have to
spend the rest of my years living within two miles of a
hospital? Would I have to give up beer? I'd hoped to go to
Czechoslovakia and write a sort of political travel book,
but I wasn't entirely keen on throwing myself on the
mercy of Eastern European medicine in the event of an attack, and I didn't fancy trying to say "Get me epinephrine" in Czech when I could barely breathe anyway.

But the more questions I asked, the fewer answers
came back. Asthma seemed to have the medical community in turmoil. A new and sympathetic view of the asthmatic was at odds with an older prejudice that lurked just
beneath the surface in some physicians as well as in the
general public: a dark stew of prejudice, contempt, irritation, distaste, a desire to have as little to do with asthmatics as possible, a fervent wish that we'd just stop
complaining and go away. The central tenet of asthma,
that it was caused by bronchoconstriction (that is, a tightening of the bands of muscle surrounding each of the airways) and would therefore best be treated by
bronchodilators (that is, drugs that relax the muscles) had
been thrown out. Now a new, cellular mechanism was
gaining ascendancy: the airways were thought to suffer
from a chronic inflammation that left them damaged,
swollen, narrowed, and so sensitive that a wide variety of

causes—allergens, chemical irritants, smoke—could make their muscles contract, their tissues swell and fill with mucus, choking the airway passages. If this were true, the actual asthma "attack" was only the tip of the iceberg, the event that we noticed above the waterline of perception, and treatment would have to address this underlying cause rather than the temporary, if alarming, attack.

This new theory had thrown the pharmaceutical world into turmoil. Old, faithful drugs such as theophylline were being called into serious question, and even the albuterol inhaler, the asthmatic's lifeline, was being viewed askance. Inhaled corticosteroids, which had been in use for some time in Europe and Canada, had suddenly stormed into the United States amid a clatter of new equipment—peak flow meters, nebulizers—I'd never heard of. From the outset I heard a background murmuring, a professionally understated but nevertheless unmistakable antagonism not only between old-school doctors and young Turks but between different branches of the profession, immunologists squaring off against allergists, and the sounds of old truths being snapped like dead sticks. If I stood my ground and asked more than four questions in a row, it became all too clear that *nobody knew what caused asthma*.

All this upheaval was squeezed into urgency by the disturbing fact that even the new, more powerful drugs and treatments seemed unable to stop a steady rise in the incidence of severe asthma, which was beginning to seem less like a seasonal malady like hay fever and more like a constant and global problem. Twelve million Americans, and 5 percent of all people in the world, have asthma. The

Centers for Disease Control and Prevention in Atlanta reported that between 1980 and 1987 the U.S. death rate from asthma rose 31 percent, and it has almost doubled in the last ten years: in 1992 nearly 5,000 Americans died of asthma. Asthma is one of the leading causes of emergency room admissions, with asthma-related health care costing more than $4 billion a year. The death rate for asthma is rising rapidly everywhere, as is the incidence of other allergic conditions such as hay fever (allergic rhinitis) and eczema (atopic, or allergic, dermatitis). Nobody knows why.

Children in particular seem to be at risk, especially black children, especially those living in inner cities. Perhaps three million children have asthma, which is the most common reason for children to miss school, and the most frequent cause of hospitalization. Childhood asthma deaths rise by about 6 percent per year. Hospital admissions for asthma almost tripled between 1970 and 1980, even though the bulk of the increase was among children, among whom black children were admitted four times as often as whites. Fifty percent of all pediatricians surveyed in 1988 believed they were seeing more asthma than they had five or ten years previously.

Here was a deeply disturbing sign that something was happening worldwide that medical science didn't understand, and that for once we couldn't hope for a miracle drug: the miracle drugs, the inhaled corticosteroids, had arrived *but they weren't the answer.*

My attack had shaken me out of what seems in retrospect to have been a steady state of denial, just as the mounting asthma mortality figures were forcing the medical profession to reconsider asthma. *You could die of this,* my attack said. Whether it was this confrontation with mortality or simply that I realized that this was a terrifying way to die, it made asthma into a present fact in my life: it was like opening the door and finding a huge UPS package on the porch, almost completely blocking the front door, with no apparent way to move it.

I wouldn't find answers to my own asthma without learning more about what was happening in the world of asthma at large, and it was possible—and presumptuous; but then I had nothing to lose—that my own asthma might hold some answers to the larger questions. Either way, ignorance had lost its patina of blissfulness; it was now just ignorance.

PART I

Possible Culprits,
Unanswered Questions

M ost illnesses are easy to blame on an act of God or an act of stupidity; in any event, they come and go, in many cases leaving us immune to them for the foreseeable future, perhaps for the rest of our lives. Asthma is chronic, and far from developing an immunity, we develop a lifelong susceptibility. The first line of treatment in asthma is avoidance. But avoidance of what? The asthmatic is doomed to gnaw on the event until he finds a clue, a cause. What did he do? What did he eat? What did he breathe? Were there feathers in the pillows? Peanuts in the sauce? In my case the narrow repertoire of skin tests had answered nothing; I still had no idea what had caused the attack. Over the next few months I haunted my own actions like a ghost pacing the scene of his own murder.

At half past midnight . . . For most of us asthmatics—excluding those of us who get asthma only when we eat peanuts, play soccer, inhale carpet-cleaner fumes, or take aspirin—asthma is worse, or worst, at night. This is the most common of observations, but still a mystery.

Sometimes it's simply that when I lie down I finally

notice that I've had a hard, dry, shallow wheeze for several hours but have been too busy or tense to notice it; the white noise of the day has drowned it out. One study showed that the mere act of lying down, laying the windpipe horizontal and exposing its length to the effects of gravity, can induce wheeze in asthmatics. (It's true: at times I've felt what seems like the weight of air on my throat and chest. Turning onto one side helps, for no good reason.) Moreover, at night we spend, say, eight hours continuously breathing in any hazards of the indoor environment: dust mites, woodstove smoke, fumes from the paraffin heater. We don't breathe as deeply or as vigorously—everyone's bronchi contract somewhat at night—and we hardly cough at all, so mucus gathers in the airways like dew, further reducing the flow of air, creating mild turbulence that is in itself an irritant. And one study suggests that anxious dreams may provoke asthma.

But the fact is that I've often felt asthma steal into my chest as the evening drew on, even if I was upright, breathing reasonably vigorously, and out-of-doors. Some suspect the body's mysterious and enchantingly named circadian rhythms. Adrenal steroids (and other hormones) are released in the early hours of the morning—I imagine dark lorries rumbling through the elegant but tangled streets of southwest London in the crepuscular half-light before dawn—and from then on their bloodstream levels gradually decrease until by evening they are virtually at their lowest, and both their anti-inflammatory and bronchodilating effects are at their weakest.

At night, a doctor-friend pointed out, illness can accelerate simply because of fear. Isolation is greatest at night; time seems longer, help farther away. Or, more simply, there's the fact that with some head colds, nasal congestion gets worse in the evening, so perhaps there is a mucus connection.

I have two theories to add to these, one borrowed, one my own. The borrowed theory is from a French researcher who describes the asthmatic as La Sentinelle—the Sentry—because he must forever watch his own disease, his own medication; and, being on guard, he has special difficulty relaxing his vigilance. Nighttime, and the approach of sleep, becomes a threat to that vigilance. The tensing sentry begins to wheeze.

My own theory—a psychological one, of course, like most lay theories, because psychology doesn't demand that we understand complex technicalities such as adrenal activity—is a more personal version of this. At various times in my life it has felt as if evening, the time of letting the day go, was the time of greatest vulnerability. Whenever I've been unsure of where my life was going, I've tended, like many people, to avoid the disturbing questions and make myself busy. What could possibly be wrong with working hard, with making oneself useful? But under those circumstances, relaxing itself becomes a threat; it raises the fear of being alone with myself, of having to face truths I have been avoiding. Sometimes I've become asthmatic, at other times I've been unable to sleep, feeling my thigh and buttock muscles refuse to unknot, as if the sentry wanted to stay on guard, checking the dark corners around the barracks, doing what he knew he did best.

In both my marriages, I developed the bad habit of hiding my dissatisfactions and not wanting to listen to my own warnings. Things will get better, I told myself, calling on that old Blitz spirit, stiffening the upper lip. Work hard, be cheerful, say nothing. Coming home, then, was like going to work; going to bed was the time of greatest tension. My throat became Pandora's box: if I relaxed my vigilance, who knew what would fly out?

... *acidic, turbulent* ... When I told my family doctor about the attack, he blamed indigestion. I was suffering, he said, from gastrointestinal reflux—in other words, the contents of my stomach were not being held in place by the cardiac sphincter but, as I lay down, were leaking back up into the esophagus.

Two sphincter muscles guard each entrance to the stomach, like Victorian governesses, to make sure that no food leaves until it has been properly digested. The cardiac sphincter relaxes to let food into the stomach, then contracts to keep it there; the pyloric sphincter crimps the passage to the intestines.

Later I watched this happen on a fluoroscope, after I had swallowed what seemed like gallons of barium milkshake flavored with sickening artificial strawberry. It was fascinating viewing. Whoever would have thought that the esophagus was so narrow and elastic, or that all our neighboring organs would be rocked back and forth by the act of swallowing? We are told, as if it were trivia, that we are mostly water, but it makes no sense until we see the liquid movements of our constituent parts. I felt like a wetland.

The concurrence of indigestion and asthma is actually quite well documented; in fact, one collection of folk remedies recommends that asthmatics avoid eating large meals shortly before bedtime. A number of experiments have treated the reflux with medication or surgery, and in general the asthma seems to improve. The question is, Why? My family doctor proposed the old-fashioned theory that the patient expressed some of the reflux (or, in laypeople's terms, brought his food back up) into the throat, breathed it in, and its acidity triggered the hypersensitive airways into asthmatic convulsion. This explanation struck me as a clunker: if this were really the mechanism, asthmatics would wheeze every time we burp, and if it were true it wouldn't speak very highly of the asthmatic's intelligence, as it implies that we would not make the connection between breathing in what would feel like scalding liquid and the immediately ensuing asthma.

The more modern theory is essentially an educated guess—namely, that repeated indigestion in some way irritates the vagus nerve, the main branch of the parasympathetic nervous system that communicates with the stomach. The vagus, which also serves the lungs, in turn irritates them, causing bronchoconstriction.

This raises a whole parliament of questions. Does the asthma precede the reflux, or vice versa? How does the overstimulated vagus nerve affect the lungs—and why should it? And does this mean that any irritation of the vagus can cause wheezing? For the vagus is named after the Latin root for wandering (as in vagrant, and extravagant) because it travels so far around the body: it runs from the brain stem to the rectum, calling at a number of major organs en route. Does this mean that irritation at any of these other stations can precipitate an asthmatic episode? And if not, why not?

To be on the safe side, I took industrial-strength antacids for two months, cut back on my workload, avoided eating after 8 P.M., and finally the nocturnal indigestion eased away. I still have no idea if my vagus nerve was to blame for my major attack—instinctively I doubt it: the symptoms were even more widespread than the peregrinations of the vagus—but if nothing else the experience had served as a warning that if I didn't take better care of my health, something worse might happen next time.

Asthma . . . But what, exactly, *is* asthma? I discovered at once that no two experts agreed, and that it's almost impossible to make any statement that is true of all asthmas or all asthmatics. Even the basic symptomatic wheeze, after which asthma gets its name (from the Greek word meaning to pant, or breathe heavily) isn't common to all sufferers: a good number cough instead.

The accepted definitions of asthma seems to have been getting steadily shorter and more inclusive, which is not a good sign. The current colloquial one—"reversible airway disease"—may seem as broad as it can get, but even that can be challenged: a 1991 editorial in *Thorax* says that asthma is arguably more a syndrome, a collection or concurrence of symptoms, than a disease. The National Asthma Education Program, called on to provide a state-of-the-physician's-art definition in its 1991 *Guidelines for the Diagnosis and Management of Asthma,* stammered twenty lines of hesitations and qualifications before enunciating a "generally agreed-on working definition," which calls asthma "a lung disease with the following characteristics: (1) airway obstruction that is reversible (but not completely so in some patients) either spontaneously or with treatment; (2) airway inflammation; and (3) increased airway responsiveness to a variety of stimuli." Nothing, you'll note, about cause.

In fact, asthma is often diagnosed by the odd logic that if you *can* find a cause for the wheezing, it probably means you haven't got asthma. You've got bronchitis, emphysema, or one of the horde of other conditions that may mimic or aggravate asthma: bronchopulmonary aspergillosis, congestive heart failure, chronic infectious bronchitis resulting from cystic fibrosis, ciliary dysfunction syndrome, upper airway obstruction, pertussis syndrome, psychogenic coughs, bronchiolitis obliterans, chronic eosinophilic pneumonia, paradoxical vocal cord dysfunction, and vasculitides. (You need not commit these to memory. Only one will reappear in these pages.)

If you're of the analytic cast of mind and you don't care for the single broad definition of asthma, you can try giving a different name to each manifestation of asthma, but that way madness lies. Dorland's *Illustrated Medical Dictionary,* 27th Edition, 1988, gives us a few dozen asthmas to choose from, including *abdominal asthma* (asthma due to pressure on the diaphragm); *allergic asthma* (also called atopic asthma); *bronchitic asthma* (asthmatic disorder accompanying bronchitis, also known as asthma convulsivum or catarrhal asthma, even though catarrh seems to be one of those diseases like consumption, or the flux, or the surfeit, which were once immensely popular but no longer exist); *cardiac asthma* (paroxysmal dyspnea that occurs in association with heart disease, also known as Rostan's asthma; this has nothing useful to do with asthma as we know it); *cotton-dust asthma* (byssinosis, a.k.a. cotton-mill or mill fever, an occupational respiratory disease of cotton, flax, or hemp workers); *cutaneous asthma* (reflex asthma believed to be caused by some irritation of the skin); *Elsner's asthma* (angina pectoris, which has nothing to do with asthma at all); *emphysematous asthma* (emphysema of the lungs attended with asthmatic paroxysms); *essential asthma* (asthma of unknown cause, also called "true" asthma; possibly the only other example of this usage of "true" is in the phrase "the one true God"); *grinder's asthma* (an occupational asthma brought on by inhaling fine particles thrown up by grinding metal); *Heberden's asthma* (also angina pectoris, which by any other name still has nothing to do with asthma); *humid asthma* (not an atmospheric condition, but simply a wheeze that is very juicy with mucus); *intrinsic asthma* (asthma attributed to pathophysiological disturbances and not to environmental factors; it was standard practice until recently to distinguish between intrinsic and extrinsic asthmas, but such a simple dichotomy is in danger of going the way of the dodo); *isocyanate asthma* (another occupational asthma, caused by allergy to toluene diisocyanate, an extremely nasty substance that will turn up later, with its cousins, in these pages); *Kopp's asthma* (laryngismus stridulus, a fancy way of saying "a noisy constriction of the larynx of no specific cause"); *Millar's asthma* (the same as Kopp's asthma; both guys must have come down with it at the same instant); *miner's asthma* (a by-product of anthracosis); *nasal asthma* (asthma caused by "disease of the nose"; this definition has clearly been held over since the first edition of *Dorland's,* published in 1445); *potter's asthma* (like steamfitter's asthma, yet another occupational asthma; there are a *lot* more of these than I've included here); *thymic asthma* ("an alleged condition," the dictionary begins, not inspiring a lot of confidence, "occurring usually in children, associated with enlargement of the thymus, paroxysmal attacks of asthma, and a tendency to sudden death"); and *Wichmann's asthma* (yet another name for laryngismus stridulus; Wichmann must have been in the bed between Kopp and Millar).

Finally, no bestiary of alleged asthmatic or pseudo-asthmatic conditions would be complete without mention of *stripper's asthma,* which, disappointingly, turns out to be another asthma associated with byssinosis and nothing to do with *sexual asthma,* asthma resulting from sexual intercourse. I actually spent much of my adolescence wondering, a little anxiously, if I would start wheezing at the height of passion, but this turned out not to be the case, luckily. In fact, I've found three references that connect asthma with sex. One claimed that orgasm involves release of histamine—note the flushed cheeks—and therefore may cause asthma. More sensibly, Thompson et al., in "Sexual Dysfunction in Asthmatics," point out that any disease that accompanies anxiety or depression and cuts your oxygen supply in half is hardly an aphrodisiac. More subtly, "Asthma patients who need to control their partners may use their illness to manipulate the sexual relationship. They may also shift from the dominant to the dependent role; this change can provoke a loss of self-esteem in the patient and cause rejection by the partner." This theory is perhaps borne out by a study of four Indian men whose asthma turned out to be caused not by sexual intercourse, as they had thought (take *that,* Dorland's *Illustrated Medical Dictionary*), but by the fear of sex. Poor bastards.

My first attack . . . Perhaps there was a clue here—or too many clues, or simple happenstances that I wanted to be clues. My first asthma attack took place in the spring of 1965, when I was eleven, on the night before a history test in the class taught by the Reverend George Emery at the Royal Free Grammar School for Boys, Worcester, England.

A year earlier, a test would have been yet another opportunity to show my teachers and my parents what a good memory I had, and what a good son and pupil I was. In the interim, though, I had moved up from the Nunnery County Primary School, a bright, new school where teachers called us by our first names and I was head boy and all-purpose top dog, to the Royal Grammar School, an ancient, dark school where everybody wore school uniforms, with strictly enforced arcane details to denote one's status in the school; and for the first time in my life my name became a mere administrative signifier: Brookes, T. My status, it was clear, was bottom dog. We were seated in alphabetical order, we had to call our teachers "Sir," and if we wanted to see a teacher in the staff room we were not even allowed to knock but had to wait outside until someone came out or went in. We suffered new punishments elicited from a book of school rules, which we had to carry at all times. The punishments were inflicted by prefects, who wore special blazers and ties, or sub-prefects, who wore no identifying insignia and were therefore a kind of secret police, and teachers, who wore academic gowns and were the strangest and most daunting collection of people I'd ever met.

Most daunting of all was the Reverend Emery. A

frightening figure, with more of the Old Testament in him than the New, he had thick black eyebrows, a receding forehead, and a protruding jaw; his scowl would have frightened the Devil. He taught Ancient History, mostly by writing on the board notes that we had to copy into our exercise books, and flying into a fury if we couldn't decipher his archaic Greek epsilons and betas. Each week he assigned a chapter from the textbook, to be learned by heart, and began the following class by going around from boy to boy, asking about dates and battles and generals. If one of us got an answer wrong, Emery would ask him two more questions. Unless he got both right, Emery would dispatch him to the front of the class to join all the other "evil boys," as he called those who had failed him, and after the test was thus administered, Emery would stalk to his desk, take out a tennis shoe, and beat them all.

My first asthma attack came in April or May. Emery, with a horrible, sideways grin, had promised us an extra-hard test—on the Punic Wars—the following day. By now I was the only boy in the class not to have been beaten. I'd studied as well as I could, then gone to bed early. I don't remember much about the attack, except that when I inhaled, my breath sounded like a church organ, and I was scared. My mother, instead of calling the Headmaster to insist that Emery be fired, as I hoped she would, reassured me that everything would be all right and sat with me until the asthma passed. The test passed, too; in fact, I studied so desperately for Emery's tests that by the end of the year I was still the only boy in the class not to have been beaten.

Our family doctor diagnosed asthma and dispatched me to the hospital's Ear, Nose & Throat Department for a battery of allergy tests, and I sat in the waiting room with eighteen needle-pricks itching and swelling on my fore-arms. The one thing they didn't test me for was allergy to history teachers.

The possible role of anxiety and a sense of helpless-ness was never brought up. The tests indicated that I was allergic, in varying degrees, to various pollens, grasses, and molds—and, oddly enough, no sooner had I been told that I had seasonal allergic asthma than, as if on doc-tor's orders, I started to sneeze and wheeze when the pollen count rose.

It was also decided that I should have desensitizing in-jections. These were not as ghastly as they sound. I didn't mind the prick of the needle, as I had decided this was an opportunity to develop mental control over pain. More importantly, every few weeks I managed to walk off with the syringe. I was fascinated by the syringes, with their high-tech calibrations, their sharp needles, and the slow driving of the plunger—an iconic action of a thousand horror shows. One day I discovered by accident that if the needle was driven through a sheet of paper it got plugged up; depressing the plunger built up the air pressure in the barrel until with a faint pop the needle shot up to six feet across the room. I had my own guided missile launcher, and under the guise of practicing the clarinet I'd hide out in one of the school's music practice rooms at lunchtime with my friend Phipps and we'd shoot at targets. The syringes gave me the kind of illicit cool that kids probably feel nowadays when they walk into school packing a .38, and it was one of only two noticeable benefits of my three years of injections, which seemed to have little or no ef-fect on my asthma, though they may have reduced my hay fever. The other was that I've never been afraid of needles since. Anything you've fired across a soundproof room at a scrawled portrait of the Headmaster tends to lose its existential terror.

My asthma was more a nuisance than a threat, and it even had its advantages: while all the other boys were out playing rugby in the freezing rain, or being sent on cross-country runs, slogging alongside the old industrial canal and up the clay banks past the factory, then back to the gym for a cold shower, I cleaned up the locker rooms. Having to wear glasses affected me far more than having asthma.

As my adolescence wore on, my breathing improved. At sixteen I went through a growth spurt, possibly delayed by the disease, and went back to playing soccer and even rugby; but after I turned twenty-one—this is true of a high percentage of asthmatics—the asthma regained its strength, becoming steadily more a part of my life, arriving a little earlier each year and staying a little longer, until by the nineties it had become a resident in my chest rather than a visitor, turning up every other night as a slight wheezy clutch at the base of the throat, like a nagging, half-forgotten anxiety.

. . . *attack* . . . Even the word "attack" is wrong, a prominent local allergist told me. Use *episode,* she says: asthma is a condition of chronic airway inflammation, so it's there all the time, whether you are wheezing or not. Once you understand this, you recognize the dormant phase, the buildup with its drop in pulmonary function, and see the acute phase as merely the culmination, the manifestation, the word made flesh.

This makes sense, I suppose, and it may help to avert some of the panic that clings to the word *attack,* but trust me: it feels like an attack. The most accurate word I can think of, actually, is *crise,* the French for "attack": it *is* a crisis, and the word's hissing exhalation, its vowel clamped down by a sibilant consonant, echoes the asthmatic's wheeze.

The whole notion of changing from *attack* to *episode* is a good example of specialists' thinking. I have met only two asthma specialists who are asthmatic, though others must exist. Moreover, while specialists see a lot of asthmatics, they tend to see us under controlled circumstances: circumstances that they control, circumstances in which the asthma is usually more or less under control. (Most allergists don't *want* to see a serious attack, or episode, or *crise.* For them, the severely wheezing asthmatic is like one of Basil Fawlty's guests, a nuisance to whom one is bound by professional necessity.) Under the unhurried circumstances of the well-decorated office, safe from the vivid anarchy of acute illness, they can tell us calmly that we experience *episodes,* and we, not currently in the grip of panic, may listen with at least half an ear, and are unlikely to punch them, or rave, or otherwise carry on in a fashion likely to bring their practice into disrepute.

The physicians who see us at our worst are the ER staff, the poor bloody infantry not long out of medical school with a fifty-thousand-dollar debt load and a second child on the way, working the ER because the pay is a little better and there's any amount of overtime. They know that ER doesn't stand for Episode Room. They may represent only the Band-Aid role of medicine—they are not experts on asthma or on us as individuals, and by restoring our breath and letting us go they implicitly reinforce the illusion that asthma is topical rather than chronic—but they know very well how terrifying asthma is, and they seem to understand far better than the specialists that fear is the counselor to whom we listen, whose terminology we use, and whose advice we take, no matter how irrational.

. . . grow out of it . . . But this is simply the most common asthma myth, the belief that the asthmatic child will "grow out of it," as if the illness were a juvenile folly, like wetting the bed. This is wishful thinking on everyone's part—the doctor's, the patient's, the parent's.

Some children do lose their symptoms between the ages of ten and twenty, though it's not clear why. Some physicians theorize that our airways broaden as we grow, going on to speculate that this might account for the persistence of asthma in adult women, whose airways are (marginally) smaller than men's. Perhaps we panic less, too, as the world becomes more familiar and predictable, and we are better able to cope with it on our own. Perhaps the hormonal changes in adolescence have some effect; perhaps our asthma eases as we move away from our parents' homes, with their psychodynamics and their indigenous allergens.

But the latest information suggests that fully three-quarters of children with moderate or severe asthma don't grow out of it. Roughly four-fifths of us still have breathing difficulties as adults, but have simply given up going to the doctor about them. Half of us use no medication at all; a quarter use medication, but usually in an intermittent and haphazard fashion—and the medication it-self may be years out of date, prescribed by a doctor who didn't check us first, or even prescribed for someone else. Fully a third of us smoke. No wonder the medical profession told us we would grow out of our illness: adult asthmatics had vanished off the medical map.

The truth is that we don't grow out of asthma; we "grow out of" taking an intelligent and determined interest in it—and, by implication, in other aspects of our health. Or maybe we simply grow out of our childhood, when our health was our parents' concern, and we stumble into adulthood blithely assuming that the diseases we've brought with us—such as asthma—are still someone else's responsibility.

If I look honestly at my own experience it seems all too likely that we behave in this apparently stupid, even suicidal fashion partly because we've been led to believe that it's a childish condition, and that sooner or later it will just go away, all by itself.

Several kinds   Asthma may actually be half a dozen conditions confused by the seductive tyranny of a charismatic onomatopoeia. I've discerned a number of differing symptoms in myself, and other asthmatics have yet other manifestations. (Physicians seem to pay remarkably little attention to such variations, though homeopaths have charted a wide array of asthmas.)

Asthmas I have noticed in myself:

• a sudden, overwhelming, massive attack like last November's, with enormous secretions of watery mucus;

34

• a gentle evening creep, with no apparent tightness or tension in the chest at all;

• moist seasonal wheezing accompanied by symptoms of hay fever;

• tension localized in the chest, with virtually no wheeze at all and no apparent grounding in anxiety (sometimes asthma disguises itself so well that I don't even realize it's there; it feels as if I'm slightly on edge, and I surprise myself by catching the echo of a faint wheeze);

• tension in the throat and neck, especially at times of anxiety;

• exercise-induced asthma, a gasping, laboring breathing (which I don't seem to have suffered from for at least fifteen years);

• cold-air asthma, with an attendant heaviness in the shoulders.

Asthmas I have seen or heard of in others:

• asthma with cough but no wheeze;

• asthma with mucus but neither cough nor wheeze;

• severe chronic asthma, a steady, constant, dry wheeze, with attendant fatigue, heaviness, bowed posture, hunched shoulders.

. . . *inhaler* . . . You'd think that here, at least, I'd be able to take one aspect of this tempest-tossed evening for granted; but asthma medications bring up more uneasy questions than ever. All asthma pharmaceuticals suffer from the problem that you can't make a useful medication for a disease you don't understand.

For ten years, before I was prescribed an inhaler, I took Franol tablets, obsolete now but at the time a standard drug in the U.K. Franol was in a sense the perfect example of basket medication—a drug that includes a little of this and a little of that to counteract the effect of the this, and then perhaps a little of the other, because it might do some good and probably can't hurt. Franol consisted of two bronchodilators (medicines that open the airways), not only theophylline but also ephedrine, plus an antihistamine, for those with allergic asthma, even though antihistamines don't do much good. But as most asthma strikes in the evening, and both theophylline (with its caffeine buzz) and ephedrine (with its adrenaline rush) were likely to keep the asthmatic awake, Franol also included phenobarbital, a long-acting sedative used in sleeping pills. Franol tablets were marked with a capital F, and my mother called them F-tabs. I hated them.

Dosing is not as exact a science as the instructions on any bottle of pills would lead us to believe. Half or even a whole tablet of Franol would sometimes have no effect after ten or twenty minutes of sitting resignedly with my feet over the side of the bed, reading if I was lucky enough to have a good book with me, otherwise just thinking. (Asthma, like hanging, concentrates the mind wonderfully.) Sometimes when this happened, I would take a second tablet, forgetting what had happened before, or hoping it wouldn't happen again, hope overcoming reason and memory. Within minutes I regretted it.

At first, my body started to feel heavy as the phenobarbital kicked in: my limbs felt abandoned, like stuffed bolsters of flesh lying here and there around me—but at the same time my pulse began to pick up and my mind started to race, taking a song phrase and repeating it over and over, throwing off images and other phrases like sparks, then going back to repeating the line, then taking up a thought and worrying it like a squirrel nibbling a nut, this way and that, too fast and fragmentary to follow it through in either a logical sequence or even the satisfying narrative of a daydream. With my leaden body and this nattering, chattering nonsense racing through my mind, it was like being trapped on the seabed in a two-man submarine with a neurotic aunt, and I would lie there for four or five hours, waiting for the drug to be filtered out of my bloodstream, dragging myself out of bed every couple of hours to take a leak, as Franol also acted as a diuretic. The following morning I was a wreck.

Theophylline, too, is an old-fashioned drug, though it is still used (probably more than it should be) as a bronchodilator. A derivative of caffeine, it delivers something of the jolt of a strong cup of tea or coffee, and thus has some of the same drawbacks as Franol. Theophylline has always had two hazards: firstly, like Franol, its therapeutic dosage and its toxic dosage butt up against each other, leaving no margin for error, and the individual's tolerance varies considerably. Secondly, if the patient has a high fever, a dangerous phenomenon called "dumping" can take place, in which the level of theophylline in the patient's bloodstream suddenly starts to rise to highly dangerous levels in as little as twenty-four hours.

Every year sees thousands of cases of theophylline poisoning, ranging from mild to fatal. To make matters worse, the FDA has different regulations for theophylline products than for products such as cough medicines that contain theophylline among other ingredients. The ABC television magazine *Prime Time Live* reported, "Each theophylline product comes with its own warnings and instructions, and there are 149 different pills and liquids on the market," such as Accurbron, Amesee, Aminodur, Amodrine, Brondecon, Bronkaid, Bronkodyl . . . (fill in another hundred or so here) . . . Theo-Dur, Theo-Dur Sprinkles, Theolair, Theolair-SR, Theophyl, Theophyl-SR, Theophyl-225, Theovent, and Verequad. By the time this book goes to press, the list will have changed. As with all drugs, the buyer must put on her reading glasses and scour the small print.

The most familiar asthma medication is in the hand-held inhaler, which delivers a dose of albuterol into the lungs. (The epinephrine inhaler, as I've said, is not generally recommended.) Albuterol is a beta-agonist: it acts on beta-receptors in the lungs, causing muscle to relax. The first time I used one of these, in 1974, I thought my prayers had been answered: instead of waiting perhaps twenty minutes for the Franol tablets to work, I could breathe normally again in less than thirty seconds.

The problem with the beta-agonist inhaler is that it is too good a temporary solution. It gives relief, but it does nothing to treat the underlying inflammation and may actually irritate the hypersensitive tissue. (Some studies suggest that constantly using an inhaler makes the worst asthmatics more likely to die of their asthma.) It also removes the incentive to understand our condition and take it seriously enough to make the radical changes that may reduce our risk of attacks. A typical asthma death takes place when an attack gets steadily worse over a day or more; the asthmatic uses the inhaler more and more frequently until the airways are so swollen and congested that it does no good—and by then the dash to the emergency room may be too late.

Our attachment to the inhaler, with which we have a strangely personal, even intimate, relationship, touches on something very deep, I think. When we're not actually suffering an attack, most asthmatics don't *feel* ill—we certainly don't like to think of ourselves as having a chronic and incurable illness—and, hoping against reason, we prefer to believe that our illness will simply go away by itself. To seek medical treatment is to admit the disease; far better to use a small, convenient, easily hidden device that allows us to be mobile and active, that can be picked up over the counter (in the case of the Primatene epinephrine inhaler) or by repeat prescription, so we never have to see the doctor and have our chronic fallibility, our mortality, exposed.

Oral prednisone, a corticosteroid, is a remarkable anti-inflammatory drug, a lifesaver. For the severe chronic asthmatic, it may be the only way to make living tolerable, or even possible. But in high doses or over long periods of time, prednisone can produce some ghastly side effects: it can delay puberty and stunt growth; it can leach calcium from bones, leading to osteoporosis and spontaneous vertebral fractures; it can cause muscle wasting, changes in skin pigment, menstrual problems, diabetes mellitus, and a general immunosuppression, which increases our susceptiblity to infection. In large doses it can also affect our moods or our grasp of reality, in some cases even causing psychosis.

Oral prednisone is a stratospheric drug: it should only be prescribed when we are in the upper levels of illness, when the benefits outweigh the side effects; and it leaves us floating, clinging to it, our feet no longer on the ground, utterly dependent on a trustworthy and available doctor and some well-informed family members.

The newer drugs try to prevent attacks rather than bail us out during our crisis. Cromolyn sodium has remarkably few side effects and, when taken regularly, cuts down the frequency and severity of many asthmatics' attacks and is especially useful for children. Perhaps because I didn't take it until I had been asthmatic for two decades, it didn't do me much good; it's also expensive. Nowadays its more effective successor, nedocromil sodium, may be prescribed instead.

The current frontline preventive therapy is inhaled steroids, sold as Vanceril, Beclovent, Azmacort, and AeroBid. Because the inhaler delivers them to the site of the inflammation, a far smaller dosage is needed than the all-out broadside of oral prednisone, and (this seems to have been a lucky accident) they seem not to leach into the bloodstream, so side effects are virtually nonexistent. Knock on wood.

Finally there's a clue, or perhaps a taunt, in the success of the most mysterious treatment of all: the placebo, an inert substance that works apparently by suggestion. In most illnesses, even cancer, if the patient is treated by someone she trusts, then either the belief that she will get better, or perhaps the simple fact that she's receiving attention, often galvanizes some as-yet-unexplained immune response, even if the treatment itself involves nothing of known medical value and should do no good whatever. Conversely, many patients have made remarkable recoveries after following what has been described to them as a "new treatment," only to relapse when they discovered that the treatment was bogus.

The placebo response is so well documented, in fact, that in pharmaceutical trials the effectiveness of new drugs is measured by how well they do compared to a placebo—after all, a new drug's success might in itself be due to the placebo effect. In one study of nedocromil sodium, the drug improved symptom scores by 50 percent, but the placebo produced 9 percent improvement, and more than half of the children, parents, and clinicians involved in the study rated the placebo as being either very or moderately effective. In a methotrexate study, taking a placebo decreased the subjects' steroid dose by 40.2 percent, and was actually *more* effective than the methotrexate.

In a sense, this information isn't much use: it says nothing about asthma in particular, and we can't wander down to the pharmacy with a prescription for a placebo. (Though many medical treatments in the past did exactly that: Tim Thompson, a doctor in Vermont's rural Northeast Kingdom, told me that one of his predecessors used to make a point of taking one pill out of every package he gave to patients, and swallowing it in front of them to show that it, and he, could be trusted. "If I did that," Tim said, "I'd be dead in a day.")

It does, however, show the enormous medical importance of trust—a quality that can be used or abused by either doctors or patients. The placebo effect enables even the most arrant quackery to work sometimes, with some patients; on the other hand, the poor fool who sucks on his inhaler every half hour, or whenever the slightest anxiety stirs, has thrown out his common sense in the name of trust, and his asthma will probably only ever get worse.

. . . *desensitizing injections* . . . This common medical response, too, is less straightforward than it seems. Skin testing for allergic hypersensitivity was first demonstrated at almost exactly the same time as fingerprint testing was introduced in criminology, during the time of Sherlock Holmes and the rise of forensic science. What hopes there must have been that such testing would identify the asthma fingerprint, would nab the intruder that stole into the body during the night!

The rise of skin testing grew from a nineteenth-century discovery that if a researcher injected allergens—grass pollen, egg albumin, horse serum—into rabbits and guinea pigs and waited a few days for an allergic sensitivity to develop, then a second injection just under the skin caused reddening and local swelling. The degree of this localized reaction, the argument went, revealed which allergens the unfortunate rodent was now sensitive to, and how violent a sensitivity it had developed. If the "allergologist" tried the same tests on humans, looked for the telltale raised weal on the skin, and then gave the patient a series of injections of small doses of the allergen serum—a treatment rather grandly called specific immunotherapy—the patient would ultimately become desensitized, and the eczema, hay fever, or asthma would be cured. Like many medical discoveries, allergy testing and desensitizing shots turned into something of a fad.

In the end, asthma turned out not to be that simple, that linear; the fingerprints it left were annoyingly blurred and inconclusive, and led to few arrests. Skin testing is still seen as one useful diagnostic tool in a physician's repertoire—tests can identify a specific culprit that the asthmatic can avoid, such as a food, or cats—but it has its limitations. In some people, the triggers are so arcane that no standard box of potential allergen serums could possibly include them (one man's asthma turned out to be triggered by the mercury in his dental fillings), while on the other hand, sometimes the allergen is so common that it is virtually impossible to avoid. Moreover, an allergen that triggers a reaction in the lungs doesn't always cause a skin reaction; conversely, scratch tests, in irritating the skin, can cause a rash (so to speak) of false positives. The desensitizing injections, too, turned out to have limited and unpredictable success (except in the case of stinging-insect venoms) and had an alarming tendency to cause the occasional death from anaphylactic shock.

The result is confusion in the public's mind and muttered controversy in the medical community. Some doctors are thoroughly skeptical of allergic immunotherapy, while at the other extreme some still carry out what has been called "remote practice of allergy"—in other words, a kind of mail-order package of skin tests and allergy shots that involves no contact between the patient and physician. We laypeople have no idea whom to believe, and as we are so used to seeing the words *asthma* and *allergy* linked with an ampersand, we mistakenly assume they go hand in hand, so we're vulnerable to such quackery. Be warned: any doctor who prescribes desensitizing injections without conducting a thorough personal examination of a patient is at best old-fashioned and at worst a crook.

What had I eaten?   The all-out, system-wide range of my symptoms suggested that I was reacting to something I had eaten. In my case, at least, inhaling an allergen affects my lungs, but digesting one produces effects throughout my body. And food is a common cause of asthma: roughly 6 percent of children have asthma caused by food allergies.

One of the curious aspects of food allergies is that the more nutritious the food, the more likely people are to be allergic to it. Eggs. Milk. Wheat. Fish. Potato. Pork. Scallops. Crabmeat. Peanuts. Beans. Peas. Almost no one, on the other hand, is allergic to diet soda or bubble gum. We are at less bioactive risk from the nutritionally inert.

. . . *Fontina cheese . . . ice cream . . .* A substantial number of people are allergic to milk and other dairy products, though this should not be confused with an *intolerance* to dairy products—that is, an inability to digest them because of a lack of the enzyme lactase. Allergy to cow's milk occurs in 1 percent to 4 percent of children, especially in twins or other multiple pregnancies, which is a puzzle. (Like all allergies, this could appear as asthma but might also turn up as eczema or severe indigestion. We still don't know why an allergic response manifests itself in different ways in different people, even within the same family.) Only about a quarter of allergic children, however, are sensitive to cow's milk alone: a substantial percentage are also allergic to eggs and peanuts, and—bad news for those seeking dairy substitutes—soy milk. Does this mean that cow's-milk allergy is actually part of some form of broader atopic condition?

Cutting cow's milk out of an allergic child's diet doesn't seem to do much to prevent the development of later allergies, and it doesn't seem to make much difference if a pregnant mother avoids cow's milk and eggs. Dairy-based baby formula quite strongly increases the infant's risk of allergic reactions, especially eczema, but only if there's a strong family history of allergies. As far as I can tell, though, I could drink milk and eat cheese until my cholesterol level hit 400 and I wouldn't get asthma. Scratch the Fontina and ice cream from the list of suspects, I'd say.

A bottle of Dos Equis and a bottle of Grolsch . . . The beer was high on my list of suspects. I've often thought that alcohol seems to aggravate an asthma-in-progress, and although I've never seen a word written about such a connection, it's quite feasible. One theory of exercise-induced and cold-air asthma points out that asthmatics have an unusually thick bed of capillaries under the epithelium—the top layer of skin cells—in our airways and suggests that a sudden assault of dry or cold air causes the blood supply first to retreat, then to return in increased force to warm and moisten the airways and prevent them suffering damage from desiccation or cold-burn. This surge of blood makes the airway tissues swell, narrowing the airway passages themselves.

Alcohol also makes us send an increased blood supply to surface capillaries; we often talk of someone being flushed or red-faced with drink. If this blood-movement affects surface capillaries all over the body, could it contribute to asthma?

In this violent an attack, though, I suspected some kind of allergic reaction. Brewing depends on yeast, a form of mold, and is notoriously prone to breeding unwanted molds of other varieties. In fact, molds can be found in beers, wines, baked goods that contain large amounts of yeast (sourbreads, pumpernickel bread, some coffee cakes), buttermilk, sour cream, canned juices and canned tomatoes, and other canned foods when not used immediately, cheese of all kinds except processed cheeses, cider, dried fruits, leftovers (especially meat and fish more than a day old), mushrooms, sauerkraut, smoked meats (including hot dogs, sausages, and corned beef) and fish, vinegar and foods that contain vinegar, such as ketchup, relishes, green olives, pickles, and mayonnaise.

I had twice had strong reactions to drinking the home-made British-style beer brewed by and sold at a pub in Burlington, and a friend who has no history of asthma or allergies remarked that whenever he drank one of their ales his throat "closed up." My skin tests have always shown me to be vigorously allergic to molds, though this one isn't an especially valuable piece of information, as there are thousands of different molds and their spores are almost impossible to count. To blame one's asthma on a "moldy basement," then, is an act of faith rather than of science.

The thought that I might have become allergic to beer in general was too dreadful to bear. Suffice it to say that I was cautiously sipping bottled beer within a couple of months of the attack, whereas a year and a half later I still haven't touched Rolaids.

Beer, like red wine, can also contain sulfites, or, to be more formal, potassium or sodium bisulfite, potassium or sodium metabisulfite, sodium sulfite, and sulfur dioxide. Sulfite sensitivity is not technically an allergy, but it is just as capable of provoking an acute attack, and it's also a concern because sulfites are used so widely: in potatoes and potato products, dried fruits and vegetables, chili mixes, hashes, chowders, some tomato sauces, syrups, toppings, dips (especially those containing avocado), seafood (especially shrimp), some potted cheese, cheese mixes, cheese paste, fruit juices, soft drinks, beer, wine, cider, vinegar, and pickles. Incredibly, until recently some asthma medications used to contain sulfites: Isuprel, Bronkosol, Metaprel multidose solutions for use in nebulizers—dispensers that produce a fine mist of medication for asthmatic children too young to use the hand-held inhaler properly—and Alupent multidoses, though the Alupent unit dose is sulfite-free. Nebulizers in general are more likely than bronchodilators to contain sulfites. Isadore Rosenfeld, in *Modern Prevention: The New Medicine*, tells a ghastly story of a sulfite-sensitive asthmatic patient who was prescribed a medication containing sulfites and . . . You don't want to know.

. . . nothing I hadn't had before . . . This may sound as if it makes sense, but in fact I'd got it entirely backward. Allergists' golden rule is "You're never allergic the first time." They argue that we go through a phase of "sensitization" that establishes the allergic response. The first

peanut, or the twentieth, or the ten thousandth primes us
to respond; the second, or the twenty-first, or the ten
thousand and first is the one that makes our throat crawl
and our breath rasp. By this logic, I should have asked myself what I hadn't eaten since.

Nobody understands why this period of sensitization
varies so much. In one house, a two-year-old develops an
allergic reaction; next door, a sixty-year-old notices, for
the first time, a shortage of breath. One survey of asthmatics visiting general practitioners in England noted the
onset of their asthma at the following ages: 41, 51, 27, 6
months, 11, 28, 27, 24, 34, 60, 11, 44, 23, 5, 12, 36,
"babyhood," 21, 60, 56, 19, 22, "babyhood," 2, 4, 14,
"childhood," 3, 16, 61, 52, 3, 33, "adolescence," 18,
"babyhood," 2, 5, 13. Adult-onset asthma seems especially severe and unpredictable, though no one's sure
why.

. . . *epinephrine* . . . Two months after the attack, Provi-
dence sent me a clue, possibly meaningless: a doctor
friend gave me a notice labeled URGENT DRUG RECALL
dated December 17, 1991, which Wyeth-Ayerst had sent
to hospitals, pharmacies, and physicians recalling more
than a dozen lots of Epinephrine Tubex syringes due to
subpotency. The lot numbers were listed and physicians
and pharmacists were instructed to "make every effort to
contact patients who may be in possession of these designated syringes." Was this why the syringe had done no
good? After all, one of the most disturbing aspects of the
attack was the thought that if it happened again, nothing I
could do would help.

The clue was a dead end. I couldn't tell if my EpiPen

had been from one of the specified lots, as I had thrown it away.

"Does this mean that doctors and pharmacists all over the country are checking their records to see who has epinephrine from these lot numbers so they can call them up and warn them?" I asked my friend.

He looked at me. "Probably not," he said dryly.

"In the car," I said   News from our Another Well-Spent Grant Department: a study at the University of Cincinnati, published in the *Journal of Speech and Hearing Disorders* in 1988, disclosed that "Asthmatic subjects increased pause time between speech segments, produced fewer syllables/breath, and spent a larger percentage of time in nonspeech ventilatory activity."

. . . aspirin . . . Everything about the attack screamed *Aspirin.* In January 1984, when I was thirty, I had just started working for the local daily paper where, in my naïveté, I assumed that my writing would be rigorously scrutinized by a hundred thousand would-be copy editors and fact checkers, ready to scribble poison-pen letters to the editor unless I turned out prose worthy of, say, Dostoyevsky. My first major assignment was to write about a husband and wife, both poets, who had both won major National Endowment of the Arts grants in the same year. I decided that in order to do them justice, I should write a piece of journalism that was as good as their poetry, and after I had read all their books and interviewed them, I had three days of working at a computer terminal in an airless building illuminated by fluorescent lights in which to do it.

By the end of the first day I had about 120 inches of

writing, some of it quite passable but with no structure whatsoever, and a splitting headache. I went home, took two aspirin, wheezed a little, used my inhaler, and lay awake most of the night imagining a structure for the piece totally unlike anything ever written, based on a series of dance movements. By the end of the second day, during which my editor told me she wanted no more than 50 inches of story, I had abandoned the dance, taken six aspirin, and used my asthma inhaler a couple of times. By the end of the third day the piece was finished, coming in at about 84 inches and filling up the entire Arts section from headline to horoscope. I went home and took my fifth and sixth, or possibly seventh and eighth aspirins of the day, and went to bed at about 9:30. Almost at once the worst asthma attack of my life took off, contemptuously ignoring several shots from my inhaler and drowning my lungs with fluid. Luckily, I was less than two miles from a hospital (eighteen months earlier I had been living in the countryside, forty minutes from town; I might not have survived an attack that far from help), and an hour later I was reeling and shaky from a generous dose of epinephrine, wondering what the hell had happened.

My first thought was that I had become allergic to the propellant in the inhaler—a frightening thought. (A Swedish study suggests that perhaps 20 percent of asthmatics are at least somewhat sensitive to propellants.) My doctor shrugged and spread his hands. A couple of days later I had another slight headache, and, suspicious of everything by now, I cautiously took half an aspirin. At once a junior version of the attack came on. Mentally crossing my fingers, I used the inhaler, and after a tense twenty minutes I was breathing sighs of relief.

Six months later, my mother came over from England for a visit, and I told her what had happened. "You've never been able to take aspirin, have you?" I asked her. "It makes you wheeze, doesn't it?"

"Yes," she said, "though I wouldn't say 'never.' It only started affecting me when I was about thirty."

Aspirin is a far more powerful drug than we usually realize. Between 10 and 30 percent of asthmatics are sensitive to aspirin, the word *sensitive* being used because the reaction doesn't seem to involve IgE, and isn't therefore technically an allergy. Those of us who are sensitive to aspirin often have no allergies at all, in fact. My symptoms—itching, flush, copious watery mucus in the sinuses and lungs, bronchoconstriction—are typical, and oddly enough, the sensitivity tends to appear in one's thirties or forties and includes all nonsteroidal anti-inflammatory drugs (NSAIDs). All in all, the aspirin-sensitive asthmatic should view the following with extreme skepticism.

Alka-Seltzer, Anacin, Bayer, Bufferin, Darvon with aspirin, Easprin, Ecotrin, Empirin, Excedrin—aspirin formula, 4-Way Cold Tablets, Fiorinal, Midol—aspirin formula, Norgesic, Percodan, Sine-off tablets—aspirin formula, Vanquish—aspirin formula, Nalfon (fenoprofen), Motrin, Advil, Nuprin (ibuprofen); Meclomen (meclofenamate); Naprosyn, Anaprox (naproxen), Feldene (piroxicam); Clinoril (sulindac); Tolectin (tolmetin), Indocin (indomethacin); Butazolidin (phenylbutazone); and possibly Yellow Food Dye #5 (tartrazine). Beta-blockers are also suspect.

Nobody knows how aspirin causes asthma. Experts in the field say things like, "At present I don't think we really know the mechanism by which aspirin induces upregulation of leukotriene generation. One suggestion is that there is diversion of arachidonic acid metabolism to the 5-lipoxygenase pathway after inhibition of the cyclooxygenase. I don't believe that that is the reason because in most cellular systems there is always an excess of arachidonic acid anyway," I've decided to wait until the jury comes back in before curling up with a good book on lipoxygenase pathways.

Instead, I'll stick with more general questions. If aspirin sensitivity is a matter of inhibiting an enzyme, why don't we react the first time we take aspirin? Why does this sensitivity appear in middle age, in fact? You'd think that if it was a sign of creeping decrepitude it would appear with increasing frequency as we enter our fifties and sixties, which doesn't seem to be the case. Would I have become aspirin-sensitive at some point anyway, or did the fact that I was putting enormous pressure on myself do anything to precipitate the sudden and total change, as if a switch had been flipped? This is the dark miracle of autoimmune failure: that one day a substance can be harmless or even beneficial, and the next it can be toxic, even fatal.

. . . *asthma is inherited* . . . Well, is it? The fact that a predisposition to asthma can run in families is so well documented as to be irrefutable. On the other hand, the exact connection between asthma and genes is fuzzy to the point of being virtually gaseous.

Some asthmas, notably adult-onset asthmas such as aspirin-sensitive asthma and occupational asthmas, seem to strike people with no family history of the disease at all. On the other hand, if parents, especially mothers, have a history of asthma, or more generally of *atopy*—that is, allergies that manifest themselves as eczema, hay fever, or asthma—the children are more likely to develop asthma than children in families without atopy, though the outcome is by no means inevitable. My mother, for example, has aspirin-sensitive asthma and is extremely sensitive to shellfish: if she goes within six feet of a cooked crab, her skin, especially around her eyes, reddens and swells. My elder sister suffers from severe hay fever; I have mild hay fever in addition to asthma; my younger sister and my brother seem to have no allergies. All of us love crab.

Asthma seems to have some genetic connection with hay fever, eczema, bronchitis, pneumonia, migraine, and—wait for it—tooth decay. Long-term asthmatic children are more likely to suffer from eczema, hay fever, bronchitis, pneumonia, and chest infections than are short-term asthmatics, which suggests that there may be some unknown but important difference between short-term and long-term asthma. Asthma, together with eczema, verbal skills, stuttering, and general disorders of the immune system, may be more common among left-handers. And how does a genetic perspective explain the fact that childhood asthma is nearly twice as common among boys as girls, but adult asthma is nearly twice as common among women as men?

This rampant confusion doesn't stop us from believing that the future of medicine lies in genetics. On March 8, 1992, the London *Sunday Times* reported that a team of British researchers, led by Dr. Julian Hopkin and Dr. William Cookson, had found the "allergy gene" that causes asthma, hay fever, and eczema. The Oxford research group used blood samples from one thousand people in one hundred families with an inherited tendency to asthma, concluding that, while the condition can be inherited from either parent, it is more likely to be inherited from the mother, who has a 50 percent chance of passing it on.

"Drugs designed to inhibit allergy-causing proteins made by the defective gene are likely to be available in a few years," the paper reported optimistically, falling into the contemporary habit of looking to genetic engineering for our future salvation. In its anxiety to see over the horizon, though, the paper then fell over its own feet by predicting that newborn babies will be tested for the presence of the gene, and positive results will "warn parents not to expose their child to . . . household dust, high quantities of pollen and dogs and cats during the first few months of life when the allergy can be 'triggered,' " a piece of advice as valuable as telling the public that they can avoid skin cancer by staying permanently indoors.

Nobody I've talked to thinks asthma is this simple.

Patient Progress Report No. 1

JANUARY 1992—The inhaled steroids made a difference almost at once. For six weeks I barely wheezed at all; then I came down with bronchitis that, as it often has, set up a particularly vicious cycle of problems that left me gasping and helpless.

The first time this happened was during my first trip to North America in 1973, when I came over to pick tobacco in Ontario—a job that, at $26 a day, paid more than any casual labor in England, and came with a work permit. I had landed in New York at the beginning of July and hitchhiked across the Midwest, my asthma as usual virtually absent when I was on the road, despite the dust and exhaust fumes. Des Moines, Boulder, San Francisco, Seattle, Vancouver, and back across Canada in four days—fine. Sleeping in new houses, old houses, parks, trucks—no problem.

Picking tobacco in the flat, sandy country on the northern shore of Lake Erie was another matter. The easiest job in the tobacco harvest is hanging the bundles of newly picked leaves in the kiln, but I took one step inside the small, high-ceilinged kiln and found it smelling so strongly of tobacco the air seemed solid, with millions of golden flecks hanging in the diagonal stripes of sunlight. I volunteered to work out in the fields instead, where you crouch under the plants to pick the biggest, lowest leaves, where the dew on the plants drenches you from head to foot and burns your eyes so badly you have to stop and curse blindly for two or three minutes, where the sap from the snapped stalks dries in your hands, arms, and head, turning into black tar, where the crop-dusting plane comes over once or twice a week to spray the fields with whatever it takes to kill the four-inch tobacco worm, a monster caterpillar that looks interesting, even amusing, until you try to pick one off your shirt and realize that you'll squash its flaccid green body before its claws let go.

Fairly soon into the six-week season I became mildly asthmatic at night and started taking Franol tablets. Within a few days I woke up wheezing and needed a tablet before we emptied a kiln, which was before we had breakfast, which was before 7:00. Soon I was wheezing again within a few hours and taking another Franol with lunch, at 11:30 or so, and then another at night, which left me lying awake exhausted with my mind speeding. The Franol exerted its usual diuretic effect, and every night I would stagger up, lurch out of the bunkhouse and quickly piss against the wall before the mosquitoes found me. By midmorning I would be breathing so hard I couldn't stand upright, and waited at the end of each row of tobacco bent over with my hands on my knees.

I took another Franol as soon as the prescribed not-more-than-every-six hours was up, then sooner and sooner, each time the wheeze returning more quickly, each pill sending my blood pressure rising, my ears buzzing, and my nerves racing until the symptoms of the asthma and the symptoms of the Franol met and I collapsed, shaking and hauling breath, on the farmer's porch. He was skeptical—it was the height of the season, a time of seven-day work weeks, and from the outside I looked reasonably healthy—but he drove me into town, where a laconic doctor listened to my chest and said, "You've got a bronchitis." He went into the pharmacy—the next room—returned with a syringe and vial, and gave me a shot of penicillin that would have cured gangrene in a horse. "Better not work this afternoon," the farmer said as we drove back in the pickup, the dust deviling up behind us.

Infection follows asthma; it also causes asthma.

I tend to get bronchitis once or twice a year, and since then every third or fourth attack has been this kind, masquerading as asthma, stealing up on me until condition and treatment meet and I am left with no option but to sit as quietly as possible and try not to breathe for a few hours until the antibiotics slowly take effect and the last batch of asthma medication drains out of my system.

Back at the present, I found myself in the usual quandary, barely able to breathe and increasingly wired from taking the inhaler at twice the prescribed rate. In despair I called my doctor, assuming there was nothing he could do but prescribe antibiotics. To my surprise and alarm he prescribed prednisone.

I had reached the final stage in the escalation of the drug war: oral steroids. Was this it, then? Had I reached the point where I would depend on high-power drugs for the rest of my life? I really, really didn't want to take it— but when I did, I lay down and slept for the first time in two days. I woke at 2 A.M., slightly giddy, a little exhilarated, the bedclothes damp with sweat, and sensed the power of the drug humming deep in my system. I felt like a small-boat fisherman on the Long Island Sound, out after dark, feeling a vibration under his feet and knowing that a pill-shaped nuclear submarine had headed out of Groton and was throbbing under him, bearing the power of life and death just beneath the surface.

PART II

Under the Skin

Meat in a Box

D uring one of my first conversations about asthma, a doctor told me of a woman who had a mysterious pulmonary complaint—persistent coughing and shortness of breath. One of his colleagues suggested that she was suffering from a variant of asthma that was so deep in the lungs that it didn't appear as asthma and didn't respond to the usual treatments.

I was surprised. I had no idea asthma could strike higher up or lower down the airways.

"It can occur anywhere there's a muscle," he said, as if that was self-evident.

I felt slow and stupid. How could I have not realized anything so basic? How could I have had asthma for twenty-seven years and still know so little about it? But wait a second, I thought; there are two entirely different realms of information here. Because medical students learn by seeing, using slides and cadavers and illustrations and photographs in medical texts, they have the advantage of a spatial understanding that enables them to see the musculature, the nerves, to make connections between the constituent systems. Seeing is enormously valuable—so valuable, in fact, we say "I see" to mean "I understand."

As patients, we "see" illness remarkably poorly. The realm of information we are given by our bodies consists of sensations, which may be as sharp as a pain or as vague as a mood, but we are not well educated in making sense of this information. The source of pain may not be where we feel the pain. Even our metaphors are unreliable. In *The Body in Question,* Jonathan Miller points out that we may speak of "a stabbing pain," even though we have never been stabbed; those who have tend to describe it in quite different terms. A friend of mine who was shot in the shoulder didn't describe it as a "shooting" pain; she thought she had been hit by a baseball.

All the same, I had a suspicion that the doctor is not the only one who had cards to bring to the table, that the patient has a kind of understanding to bring to this process, too. After all, if I have a chronic illness I live with it. My illness and I become a pair of mismatched explorers deep in the jungle, far from human habitation. My own perspectives and hypotheses may be little more than superstitions at times, but at least they are the best guesses from someone who has been on hand willy-nilly, all those years, the one who has hacked through enough jungle beside this bastard to have earned the right to my own opinion.

Yet I found that trying to talk to a doctor in his language, on his terms, I felt ashamed and ignorant. I had to see a lung.

Two months later, I met Dr. Larry Coffin, a thoracic surgeon at the Medical Center Hospital of Vermont who had agreed to be my tour guide. He stood at the desk outside the operating rooms, the public-go-no-farther. He was short, bespectacled, middle-aged, sandy. He was wearing a scrub suit with his mask hitched up on top of his head, and at once I wondered if I'd recognize him the following day, in his street clothes.

He found me a locker and gave me instructions: Strip to underwear, put on scrub suit. No need to scrub up, as I wouldn't be touching anything. Bootees over my sneakers; hair net, mask.

We paused outside the O.R. while the patient was being put to sleep, and Larry and his assistant, Dr. John Pietropaoli, went over the case. I glanced through the window of the other O.R. and was struck by the scene: for reasons I couldn't put my finger on, it reminded me of a railway station. Half a dozen gowned figures were moving around, not exactly aimlessly but without an apparent sense of crisp, urgent purpose. Only the surgeon was at the operating table, bending over the patient, invisible under several layers of blue hospital drape—bending over surprisingly far, as if he were playing Santa and reaching into the bottom of a deep sack for the last few presents.

It was time for us to go in to our own operating theater. I caught a glimpse of the patient, an eighty-one-year-old priest, lying on his back on the table. Two wide-bore clear plastic tubes disappeared into his mouth, pulling his lips back: I could see the fillings in his molars—and, a few minutes later when they turned him on his side, the wrinkled skin of his buttocks. These were the only two features of his reality as a human being that stayed with me over the next three hours.

Larry took me over to a wall where two X rays and

thirty-six smaller black-and-white CAT scans were mounted and lit. In the X rays, the lungs had several white spots, and I expected one of these to be the tumor, but in fact they were harmless calcified granulomas and cysts— the patient had them all over his body, Larry said: lungs, kidneys, thyroid. A lifetime of smoking had left him riddled with these harmless chunks of matter and with emphysema, a chronic lung disease that leaves the airways, normally pliant, sooted up like a chimney and clumped together. This reduces the total surface area of the lungs and thus their efficiency, forcing the patient to breathe harder to get the same amount of oxygen. I imagine emphysema to feel like permanent acute asthma; I didn't envy him.

As Larry and John talked about the priest, I was struck at once by the fact that to them he was no longer a priest but a patient, and in losing his calling he had also lost his right to pronouns: Larry referred to the arms, the lungs, the chest cavity. The priest had become the definite article, a subject in the process of becoming an object. Actually, since I was a first-timer in the O.R., this was okay by me: before this was all over I might be glad of a little emotional distance. I wondered if the priest had prayed the previous night and whether anyone was praying for him now.

I concentrated on the CAT scans, a series of cross-sections of the patient that started at the neck and worked down a couple of inches at a time. The first section contained the white epaulette shapes of his shoulders, and the black spot in the center was his windpipe. In the second or third his lungs appeared as dark pools with lighter swirls, as if someone had poured black ink into clear water. The blackest spots were the alveoli clogged with emphysema; one of the light spots was the tumor, in the right upper lobe. In with a needle, out with a few cells for biopsy—at eighty-one, surgery. In the bottom CAT section the body was almost round, the lungs filling most of the chest, leaving space in the center for the heart: they looked like two steaks on a plate.

The two anesthesiologists were chatting with a colleague who had dropped in. "So she bled all night, huh? I kinda suspected that from the way she was oozing. . . ." The priest's large, flaccid stomach rose and fell very slowly. The nurse brought John two bowls with swabs, and he carefully dabbed Betadine, an antiseptic that contains iodine, all over the priest's side, where the cut would be made. Under the lights the liquid was a shiny yellow-brown: John looked for all the world as if he were basting a turkey.

Larry was going to try a thoracoscopy. "This is what's called VATS: Video-Assisted Thoracic Surgery," he said, then added in a dry aside to the nurse, "I don't know if we're going to be able to live through this"—this much change, he meant, this much novelty. It was like the arthroscopic surgery I had had on my knee: the advantage is that the exploratory work is done without having to cut a huge incision that takes time and pain to heal and leaves a legacy of scar tissue just where you want it least. They would make two cuts, each as wide as a finger, one for a metal sleeve through which they'd slide the camera, the other for any tools they'd need for probing and cutting. They donned light clear-plastic visors, which made them look like white-collar welders, and it was time to get under way.

The first surprise was the cutting itself, which, after an initial shallow scalpel incision that for some reason did not bleed, was done by high-voltage electricity. The tool looked like the hot-wire cutter used for cutting Styrofoam: instead of producing blood, it produced smoke. Within a few seconds John had his fingers between two ribs and was poking through the chest cavity as if through lard. By now the priest had disappeared entirely beneath the drape, and our focus was in any case not on him as a person. There was no evidence of personality here, which was as it should be: Larry was now seeing thorax as a dentist sees teeth, and the priest's survival might depend on his doing so. The camera, which rather disturbingly resembled a high-tech basting syringe, was hooked up to the monitor, its light-source plugged in on the side of the syringe. Larry slid it into the metal sleeve, looked up at the monitor, and we were in a new world.

The lungs looked nothing like the photographs I'd seen of corallike alveoli waving pinkly in darkness. Everything on the screen had the clearly defined curving soft geometry of organs on a butcher's slab, each covered with a glistening membrane, making up a landscape of remarkable color: the lung, partly deflated but still beating and trembling, was pink and purple with clusters of black speckles—carbon, John explained, the deposit of a lifetime of breathing the air of our outside world. Even nonsmokers' lungs look like this. Fat, slithering in the crevices between the lungs and the chest wall, was yellow; the insides of the ribs were glazed yellow on white, with thin, branching, ruddy veins. A few drops of green fluid were pus, Larry explained: I was amazed to know that I might recognize something in here. John poked into the second hole, and we saw the bulge his finger made. A few seconds of hot-wire work, and the screen suddenly went opaque with smoke. A minute later the jaws of a probe suddenly appeared from the bottom of the screen like a metal crocodile breaching.

Only the smallest trickle of blood could be seen, a brook on a soft alien planet. (The less blood present, the greater the surgeon's skill.) What an odd thing blood is, or rather bleeding is. I think of my body as being full of blood, the slightest nick or scrape releasing it, but here we were, prodding and poking around the body's core, and the only blood in sight seemed to have come from the entry wound. But each packaged organ is, of course, gorged with blood—and realizing that, I understood for the first time what it means to say that the skin is an organ, sealed, with its own blood supply. Slice it and it bleeds, as would the lungs, or the heart, or the liver. The difference is that we can see it.

Larry explained that a strange arch of tissue was an adhesion: some ancient injury or infection, possibly tuberculosis, had left one of the lung's three lobes stuck to the chest wall with scar tissue. He slid the hot-wire through the metal tube, applied it to the arch, and sparks flew—a thoroughly unexpected sight. Under its membrane, the adhering tissue was nasty-looking stuff, green and granular. Larry burned through it, and the lobe, with a little crest of charred flesh, was released, and collapsed slowly towards its natural rounded shape. It was ten past ten. We'd been in here barely an hour and my back was already aching. How did these people do it?

But the search for the tumor was not going well. The new electronic tools are difficult to manipulate; it's like playing video games in a mirror. "Gizmos and gadgets," John sighed. The tumor was too far in and, besides, the best way to find it is by touch: it would feel like a small squash ball, or perhaps a grape, Larry said. He abandoned the new technology. "I'm going to do a thoracotomy." The metal sleeves were withdrawn, leaving no blood, just soft-sided holes in the priest's chest like ancient bullet wounds in pork.

Now the long incision was needed, around the side of the chest virtually from sternum to scapula. Retractors like stainless steel pasta forks pulled back the open white rubbery fat down to the cut flesh. The nurse laid out four bundles of black surgical thread and covered them with a cloth. The anesthesiologist deflated the lung to be examined—this was why two tubes ran into the priest's mouth, Larry explained: they could inflate or deflate the lungs independently—and John inserted four metal brackets that held the incision open, spreading apart the ribs, which must be remarkably elastic to cope with such abuse at the age of eighty-one. The result was a hole about four inches square. John donned a headlight like a miner's helmet, beckoned me up from behind him, and we looked in.

It was perhaps the strangest sight I had ever seen. The priest was lying on his left side, and with his right lung deflated, the chest cavity was half empty. Who would have expected so much space inside the human body? There was a cavity—a well-lit, orderly-looking cavity—bigger than a gallon milk container, and at the bottom was the deflated lung, lying limp and purple on its active partner. *Like meat in a box,* I found myself thinking, stunned at how something so amazing could look so ordinary. *Like meat in a box.* John fingered the deflated lung and then dropped it; it fell limply. I couldn't get over my astonishment at the human body: the lungs have a surface area the size of a tennis court, yet this was no more than a cupful of tissue. Earlier, I had fears of fainting or throwing up; instead, I was reeling in sheer wonder. I felt like a kid who had voyaged with Marco Polo, back with his family at last, exhausted, battered by their questions, sitting down and taking a deep breath, his mind full of shapes and colors he knew he would diminish by naming.

Larry, by contrast, was simply spending a day at the office. "Under my thumb . . . the size of a grape . . . deep in the lobe . . . I'm going to do a lobectomy." The supervising nurse came in with clean drapes and stayed to empty the garbage bags. A student appeared, was welcomed, peered into the cavity, and was asked to hold a clamp. One of the two anesthesiologists had left an hour ago; the other glanced at the EKG every few minutes when an irregular heartbeat or two went pong-ping-pong instead of pong-ping, but otherwise lounged on his elbows at the head of the table, peering in like a passerby at a construction site. The surgeons had only twice moved with any sense of urgency, once when tying off and cutting this branch of the pulmonary vein, once when doing the same with the pulmonary artery. Otherwise, this was a procedure. They proceeded. The meat in the box was patient, compliant.

This was not television. Nobody was fighting for life here, simply being careful. If anything, a surgeon's job is dangerous in being too easy. He's not a general practitioner facing an abusive patient or a nurse with vomit or diarrhea all over her uniform. Being a surgeon is an exercise in not abusing absolute power. His job is to know his territory and his materials, to measure twice and cut once, as they say of carpenters. Being tall, I was asked to help move one of the big lights that had stuck—"watch your pants on the table, there"—and it occurred to me that much of what goes on in the O.R. is on this level: do the small, mechanical thing, know what is where, keep the area sterile, don't knock things over. This was not *Emergency Ward Ten*. It was the railway station.

We were now two and a half hours into the operation. The careful stapling, tying off, cutting went on. What an odd thing it is to cut into a priest's chest, like Sir Thomas Browne dissecting a sparrow to see if he could find its soul: would we find his faith? A whimsical, romantic, even a contrived question—but perhaps it wasn't so ridiculous, because for the last half hour I'd been aware of how reassuring this was, watching the operation at work, how much less frightened I'd be the next time I had to be in here, how the terms *tumor* and *operation* had become more, well, operational, more mundane. Perhaps a kind of faith is to be found in here after all.

At 11:45 I murmured my gratitude and left. Things were still going on, but I had set up a game of tennis over the lunch hour. I remembered it guiltily at first; it seemed sacrilegious. Then I thought of the priest with his emphysema, his lifetime of smoking, and I knew that this was the best thing I could do for my own lungs. As I ran over to the gym it seemed to me that I had never breathed so easily, my heart had never pumped so well.

Mythology Barrier

The operating room had made medical science fascinating—a quality that, I was beginning to think, had value of its own in the process of my becoming an Informed Patient—but I hadn't learned much about asthma. Even peering in between the priest's ribs I was still seeing the lungs from the outside. His lungs were inflated or deflated; nothing else. In fact, I was still seeing them as lungs, as if lungs were single, whole things in themselves rather than complex civilizations consisting of vast numbers of cells. And if I was right about the way in which our understanding depends on what we can see, then I needed to break though a kind of metaphor stratum, to get down to a new way of seeing things.

Until now, if I'd thought about cells at all I'd assumed they were rather inert units of construction, like individual kernels in an ear of corn. As I started reading about them, discovering that cells have cytoplasmic organelles, consisting of, among other things, mitochondria, an endoplasmic reticulum, and a Golgi apparatus, I found myself in a landscape of mutant mythology, half science and half rampant science fiction, the semisensical delirium of a Flash Gordon episode.

"Zarkhov! The mitochrondia are threatening to engulf us! Engage the Golgi apparatus!"

"But, Flash! The gamma interferon is driving them crazy! They're wrapping their organelles around the ship's peptide chains! They're after the Substance P! We *must* give it to them!"

Wait a minute, I thought. Something odd was going on. Even though I had every intention of learning about the cellular mechanisms of asthma, as soon as I started reading, my mind slid off the subject and started converting science into science fiction, like a rebellious thirteen-year-old in his first biology class. But what was science fiction, if not an attempt to convert the latest discoveries of science into human terms—to translate them, so to speak, into mythology we already believed in?

This curious sensation seemed to fit in with something else I'd begun to notice about the mythology of medicine. Virtually all conversations about illness are conducted on the level of folk belief and mythology—and I'm not talking about the small percentage of poor souls who take every word of the *National Enquirer* as gospel. We simply have no idea what we're talking about most of the time. It's not that the average person is stupid or can't handle information or analysis. As Noam Chomsky has pointed out, when it comes to sports, ordinary people have long and intricate conversations with a high degree of thought and analysis. They know all sorts of complicated details and have far-reaching discussions; they have their own opinions and speak with confidence. When we talk about medicine, though, we do so at a level of superficiality that is astounding.

(This represents yet another failure to make responsible and imaginative use of television. Where is the David Attenborough of the cell? Where is the twelve-part BBC/Time-Life series called *Disease and Health* that shows us the stunning inner landscapes of the body?)

All mythologies are a way of talking about the inexplicable in terms that we can understand, even if they are not entirely accurate: fear of the unknown is a greater imperative than a scrupulous desire for accuracy. The more important a subject and the less we know about it, the more necessary the mythology—and it would be hard to find another subject as important as health that we understand so poorly. Asthma, like most illnesses, has its mythologies—and, frankly, medical science would do well to try to understand these while it tries to understand which chromosome houses the asthma gene—but it was time to drag myself beyond them. I needed to crash through what I had begun to think of as the mythology barrier.

For the next few weeks, as I struggled with lymphocytes and macrophages and platelet activating factor, it became increasingly clear why the mythology barrier exists and how important it is. I began to think of it as the energy barrier that surrounded the galaxy in *Star Trek,* which was so vivid and daunting that it was said that no spaceship could cross it without being destroyed: it served to keep us in, but also to protect the galaxy from marauders. It's a form of ignorance, of course, but it's also a form of protection from the endless darkness of the unknown, which may turn out to be a million times vaster than the small plot of earth we understand.

The value of this barrier came home to me as I spent more and more time on the other side. It was virtually impossible not to see the medical galaxy as an almost entirely alien civilization, with its white uniform, its arcane language, and its lofty disdain for the customs and myths I had brought from my own world, which seemed Neanderthal in comparison. My Golgi apparatus jokes were, for a while, a necessary way of maintaining some sense of identity in the face of so much new information, such an entirely different series of perspectives, and such certainty, delivered at times with a faint whiff of scorn.

The barrier began to crack not when I could recite the five kinds of antibody but when I realized that I was merely exchanging one mythology for another. After all, even scientists have to name things in terms of what they know. All macrophage means is "big eater," to the microphage's "little eater." The only difference is that the medical world coins its words in ersatz Greek. And the mythology barrier collapsed completely when I discovered that the certainty of the new world, which had seemed as powerful and ubiquitous as gravity, was a front. If I, like a four-year-old, asked the specialists "Why?" five times in a row, *everybody was stumped*—and in most cases, it seemed, was glad to let go of the pretense of being all-knowing, to fess up to being just another working stiff trying to put the kids through college by doing bronchial biopsies and trying to figure out why the hell asthmatics should have a thick layer of collagen underneath the epithelial cells lining the airways.

From then on I saw myself as a kind of trader, passing back and forth between mythologies, and as long as I didn't try to discuss eosinophil recruitment over dinner at home, I could make progress: from now on, my only limitation was lack of knowledge. But this struck me as a valuable, even a crucial, period of learning about how and why medicine does and doesn't work. It's perfectly possible for laypeople to resist, to an almost insane degree, the chance to learn about health and illness; but it's equally possible for physicians, who were once on the same side of the barrier as we, to forget the customs and the language they grew up with, and even to think that, just because their mythologies are denser than ours, they are therefore the truth.

Gospel Truths

I t took almost no time at all, in fact, to realize that some of the ways in which asthma had been authoritatively explained to me were as full of holes as a Swiss cheese caught in the St. Valentine's Day Massacre.

Until as recently as the late 1980s the official version maintained that there were two kinds of asthma: extrinsic (asthmas that were a response to some outside force or agent) and intrinsic (anything that didn't seem to be extrinsic). The explanation of extrinsic asthma is dramatic and colorful and was solemnly memorized by many generations of medical students who were probably not encouraged to point out that it left large numbers of questions unexplained. It goes like this:

We say good night and go up to bed. The room is a little dusty, the mattress and blanket are a little old, and all are full of dust, which in turn is covered with dust mites, perhaps a thousand of them per gram of dust. We lie down and start breathing them in.

Our airways have a remarkably efficient means of catching large airborne particles. The trachea, the bronchi, and the larger airways of the lungs are lined with mucosal cells and hairlike cilia, which beat in a steady up-ward motion. Pieces of soot and dust, fragments of leaf and feather, the kinds of specks that are large enough for us to see floating in a sunbeam, land on the cilia or stick to the mucus, are passed upward, and find themselves ejected whenever we clear our throats or cough. (Curi-ously, in the presence of infection or allergens the cilia beat more slowly.)

Smaller particles—pollen grains, mold spores—are more of a problem. Drawn by the negative air pressure created by the expanding lung cavity and the lowering di-aphragm, thousands of minute specks of dust and mites flow down the trachea as if it were as wide as the Missis-sippi, pass into the smaller and smaller branches of the lungs, and end up in the alveolar sacs, the tiny globes of lung tissue wrapped in capillary blood vessels, where the inhaled air is so close to the bloodstream that the oxygen atoms in the lung can react with the hemoglobin in the blood to create oxyhemoglobin, which will return along the pulmonary veins to the heart, before being pumped out on its arterial journey throughout the body, deposit-ing its load of oxygen wherever it is needed. The alveoli are so small that there is no room for cilia, and mucus would be a gummy disaster. The airways' main defenses ended some way back up the pulmonary tree, and down here in the small twigs the dust mite lands right on the naked lining of the airways, the epithelial cells.

The epithelium is in a sense the skin of the lungs, but it isn't the smooth, featureless, pink expanse that we might imagine; for here at the cellular level everything is very small, very crowded, and very busy. Within a few minutes the mite may receive a visit from the first player in the astonishingly sophisticated orchestra we unimaginatively call the immune system: a macrophage.

A macrophage is a humble-looking brute, resembling, perhaps, a glob of snot. It rolls over the cell mite, feeling it as a blind person might feel the face of a stranger, and at once it can tell by the molecular structure on the surface of the intruder that this is not one of the several hundred thousand different cells that are part of the human being in whose bone marrow the macrophage was created: it is *non-self.* This is the basis of what we think of as identity. The macrophage is a xenophobe, killing anything that seems foreign; death, in this sense, is a liquefaction of self.

The macrophage is in itself a powerful defensive cell: perhaps 90 percent of invading organisms, known as antigens, are destroyed by macrophages (and other scavenging cells) before any other aspect of the body is aware of the invaders' existence. (*Allergen* differs from *antigen* in that it refers to an invading substance that, even though it provokes an excessive immune response, actually represents no threat to the body: the danger comes from our own overreaction.) The macrophage immediately destroys the mite, engulfing it and secreting enzymes that dissolve it. But the immune system has learned the hard way, over thousands of centuries, that invaders seldom come alone: a simple infection may flood the tissues and the bloodstream with hundreds of thousands of bacteria, every one of which must be killed if the self is to survive. So the macrophage takes a fragment of cellular debris from the destroyed mite and awaits the arrival of a particular kind of lymphocyte called a helper T-cell.

Although the body has billions of T-cells in circulation, this isn't as easy a task as it may seem. The macrophage is moving more or less at random, borne along by the circulation of the lymph, and it isn't looking for just any T-cell. It is looking for a T-cell that has a receptor on its surface that fits the molecular configuration on the fragment of mite that it has saved.

The letter *T* stands for thymus. Although our lymphocytes, or white blood cells, are manufactured—at the rate of a billion a day—in the bone marrow, they are yet not trained for their specific tasks. About half of the immature lymphocytes pass through the thymus, at the base of the neck, where they acquire specific properties and functions. Each emerging T-cell is specific to one antigen or non-self molecule—in other words, of all the roughly hundred million possible invading entities that its host human might encounter, *or any human might encounter in the history of the race,* each T-cell is specifically adapted to be alert for and to deal with just one.

(At this point in my medical education I kept being struck by the vast numbers involved, and the sense that health is, above all, multiple. A billion lymphocytes being formed a day; a single virus cloning ten thousand copies of itself overnight, and all this activity taking place without my conscious control. . . . Instead of thinking of my brain as the master and my body as the slave, I began to think of myself as an *aggregate* entity, a sort of suburban sponge. I felt almost like referring to myself as "we.")

The macrophage, then, is looking for one specific kind of T-cell designed to combat the threat it has encountered. Evolution has developed a remarkable way of making the macrophage's needle-in-a-haystack search easier. Although the adult human has some 2,000,000,000,000 lymphocytes, only about 1 percent are in the bloodstream at any given time. The rest are concentrated in a number of tissues—bone marrow, the spleen, the lymph nodes, the tonsils—each of which consists of such a delicate and skillfully connected network that in a short period of time the macrophage rubs up against a large number of T-cells in an orderly manner. It's like hitchhiking on a freeway: instead of hanging around at the roadside, hoping for the right car to come along, it makes much more sense to go to a rest area and wander from picnic table to picnic table asking if anyone is going to Tuscaloosa, or Basingstoke, or St.-Etienne.

Finally the macrophage, feeling the surface of one helper T-cell after another, finds one with a receptor the same shape as the molecular structure of the mite, and clamps onto it. At once the T-cell, hitherto inert, is activated. It begins to clone itself, and it releases a chemical signal to another kind of T-cell to begin killing any host cells that may have become infected by intruding bacteria (or other invaders). In fact, a stunning variety of kinds of communication is by now beginning to take place among a large number of players in the immune orchestra, many of which are still not understood and most of which need not concern us here. What is of importance to the development of allergies is that chemical messengers called cytokines set out from the helper T-cell bearing the molecular signature of the antigen—like a prison guard carrying a shred of the escaped prisoner's clothing to the bloodhounds—to a B-cell.

B-cells, which are produced in the bone marrow, are a second type of lymphocyte, whose role is not to attack antigens but to produce immunoglobulins, or antibodies, that are designed specifically to lock onto one particular antigen or allergen. This is the beginning of what is called specific, or acquired, immunity. The B-cell remains inert until it has received word from the T-cell that its target antigen has been recently found in the area *and* it has itself come into contact with another such antigen. (This confirmation system, like the two-key nuclear launch commands, is typical of the immune system's caution: its defensive toxins are powerful enough not only to kill viruses and bacteria but to do extensive damage to the body's own tissues, so it usually releases them only under highly controlled circumstances. Imagine fighting a war on one's own soil in which the defensive side was as concerned about protecting its own civilization and environment as it was about destroying the enemy. We'd need weapons a damn sight smarter than we have at the moment.)

Thus alerted, the B-cell divides and multiplies, evolves into a plasma cell, makes enormous quantities of antibody—billions of molecules per cell per hour for three or four days—and dies.

Antibodies are very, very small. There are five classes of antibody: IgM (for Immunoglobulin M), IgG, IgA, IgD and IgE. Each has a different shape and a different function. IgM, for example, is a very large molecule that consists of a hub like an airport terminal with five arms radiating outward, each of which branches into two binding sites. Each IgM molecule can therefore in theory bind to up to ten bacteria, but in practice bacteria are so much larger than the antibody that the IgM molecule hangs on like a spider clinging to a barrage balloon. The clustering of bacteria and antibody, though, creates a large target that is easily recognized by the next waves of the immune response, the larger granulocytes and macrophages that are good at destroying aggregations of invasive material. IgM's limitation is its size: being so large, it is confined to the bloodstream, so we need smaller antibodies that will be drawn between the cells in the capillary wall and attack bacteria in the tissues themselves, destroying it by binding to it and drilling holes in its outer membrane.

If this is the first time I have come into contact with mites, then whoever I am, whatever my family history of allergies, the first antibodies I will make are all IgM, whose agglutinating abilities make it an ideal first-line response. After a while, the genetic instructions encoded in my DNA will conclude that enough IgM has been made for the time being, and will instruct the B-cells to start producing one of the other classes of antibody, usually IgG. These are the battle-tested troops, the standard military response. IgE usually plays a minor role: in most people, probably only 1 percent of the antibody produced is IgE. In some of us, though, the genetic instructions the B-cell receives are different: produce IgE, they say. Early and often. Perhaps ten, even twenty times as much as usual.

This is an odd response for the simple reason that IgE seems to do a damn sight more harm than good; in fact, it's hard to discern what good, if any, it does. (We don't know what good IgD does, either.) One theory is that our dust mite has the same molecular blueprint as some dangerous parasite long extinct, and our immune system galvanizes itself into a panic over an enemy that no longer exists. Other theories can form a line over by the door.

In itself, IgE, even in abnormally large amounts, is not a problem. In the constant war on viruses, bacteria, and other antigens, it isn't even, strictly speaking, a weapon. Each IgE molecule looks rather like an aggressive letter Y, perhaps one that has cross-bred with a lobster. At the tip of each arm is a pair of pincers, which, remarkably, have been custom-made: *They are specifically designed to lock onto the protruding molecular formations on the outer surface of the mite that the macrophage encountered and destroyed.* But the IgE doesn't just flood into the bloodstream looking for mites: on its own, it would do virtually no good. Instead, it enlists the help of a mast cell.

The function of the mast cell, as of most players in the immune system, is to contain an infection: if it is informed of clear and present danger, it marshals all our defenses to minimize the spread of the invader. Because of the way in which they are distributed, mast cells can also be thought of as gatekeepers: for bacteria and viruses, the easiest access to the body is through the mouth, nose, and skin; and mast cells are found in greatest concentration lining the surfaces beyond these ports of entry—namely, just under the surface of the skin, in the nasal passages, the lungs, and the intestines.

The IgE molecule, so tiny it can barely be seen with an electron microscope, will feel its way around the epithelial region until it encounters a mast cell—which won't be hard to find, as the mast cell is moored to the epithelial wall and is about a million times larger than the immunoglobulin molecule. At this point, it's hard to avoid thinking in terms of the graceful maneuverings of space vessels in Stanley Kubrick's *2001: A Space Odyssey,* for the tail of each IgE molecule is a form of docking mechanism.

The surface of the mast cell is pitted with as many as a hundred thousand receptors, and once the IgE molecule docks, the mast cell is primed.

In this theater of chemical warfare, the mast cell is a cross between a frontline radar dome and a land mine. Just large enough to be seen by a powerful light microscope, it looks like a raspberry overstuffed with seeds. Each seed is a granule of chemical mediators, each of which will either carry out a function that will help in the fight against infection, or instruct another player in the immune system to do so. The most common ingredient is histamine, which makes small blood vessels expand, so the cells in their walls no longer fit together as snugly, and lymphocytes can slide between them out of the bloodstream and attack antigens in the surrounding tissue. This leads to swelling, which also narrows the airways, and an accelerated production of mucus, which clogs them still further. Histamine also makes the smooth muscle that is wrapped around our airways contract; this is bronchoconstriction.

The IgE molecule is now docked on the surface of the mast cell, along with hundreds or thousands of other IgE molecules, some specific to cat dander, some to pollens, some to molds, as our genetic predisposition to overproduce IgE has probably sensitized us to a variety of allergens. Its two claws reach out into the intercellular space in the epithelial or mucosal tissue. This is the device that will alert the mast cell to clear and present danger.

Why are some people more sensitive than others and suffer more potent allergic reactions? It depends on whom you ask. The more one is exposed to an allergen, the more IgE specific to that allergen is present on the surface of the mast cells, and therefore the more sensitive the individual—or so some allergists believe. Sensitive people may have slightly more mast cells than nonsensitive people, and mast cells may migrate a little toward the surface in sensitive people's lungs, but by and large the mast cell is fairly constant and fairly static—certainly compared to its other granular cousins, the basophils and eosinophils, of whom we'll hear more when we start hearing the immunologists' version of things.

A week, or a month, or a year later, we are in bed again, inhaling thousands of dust mites. Before long, mite particles blunder up against mast cells. In some people, this would be a harmless, random event, for the mites pose no threat to us; but we asthmatics are by now sensitized to mite, and the molecular structure on its surface fits exactly into the pincer-like antigen-binding site at the end of one arm of one of the thousands of mite-specific IgE molecules on the surface of the mast cell—or, more likely, many fragments of mite bind to many IgE molecules on many mast cells. At once, things begin to happen.

Cell biology is still working on letting us know how information about events at the surface of a cell is sent to the nucleus, but a messenger system involving chemical reactions reprograms the nucleus of the mast cell, which immediately makes its own cell wall rupture, and the granules rush out, leaving the mast cell looking like a punctured basketball. The inflammatory mediators in the granules start up the classic inflammatory response— swelling, mucus production, smooth muscle contraction—reducing the air flow and making us wheeze or cough.

If histamine were the only chemical agent involved, and its only effect to cause the airways to contract, then it might make medical sense to treat asthma with bronchodilating inhalers or pills, or even antihistamines. But this is not the case, and, besides, such a reaction would make no sense from the immune system's point of view. The mast cell is in the business of protecting against potentially fatal invasion, so it alerts an entire arsenal of defenses. Other players, notably prostaglandins and leukotrienes, contribute to those powerful local effects, and still others send out distress messages that summon neutrophils and eosinophils, which arrive over a period of hours or even days, prolonging the inflammation and creating what is known as late-phase asthma even after the original stimulus has gone.

Much of this explanation is probably true, and all of it may be true for some asthmatics, but it leaves enough questions to fill the telephone book of a small city. If, for instance, we have mast cells in various tissues (nose, lungs, skin, gut), and as far as we can tell IgE doesn't discriminate between them, why are allergic reactions specific to one tissue? Why do we have hay fever in the nose, not in the lungs? Why do we have eczema on the skin, not in the alimentary canal? Why do people start wheezing when there are no allergens around—in cold weather, for example, or under emotional pressure, or during exercise, or when they laugh?

In order to answer—or perhaps to pigeonhole and then forget—some of these questions, the notion of intrinsic asthma was invented. I thought I was merely being a bit dim in being unable to understand the exact mechanisms of intrinsic asthma until a pulmonologist handed me a photocopied page from a medical textbook. This didn't tell me much about asthma, but it told me a great deal about medical education.

The part of the page depicting extrinsic or allergic asthma was suitably graphic—mast cells puncturing, releasing little dots of histamine, epithelial cells overflowing with mucus like effervescing champagne flutes—but the intrinsic part, headed "Nonimmunologic Mechanisms," was oddly short of artwork that actually meant anything. All it had was an arrow leading to "automatic pathways" (whatever they are), another arrow leading down from a list of chemical mediators, a strange and frankly ambiguous horseshoe-shaped arrangement of lines branching to the phrases "alpha adrenergic" and "beta adrenergic," both of which were prefaced by tiny arrows not pointing at anything in particular—and then, like the hero leaping in to rescue the maiden tied to the railway tracks, another arrow boldly pointing to a picture of a swollen, constricted asthmatic airway.

I couldn't help thinking that the word SOMEHOW must have been written across the diagram in invisible ink over this last, skeletal explanation. Where are the hectic but informative pictures of the nonimmunologic mechanisms affecting the autonomic pathways, or of the urgent meeting between the mediators and the pathways, like Cyrus Vance, David Owen, and a congregation of variegated Serbs, Bosnians, and Croats meeting at some blighted roadside near Sarajevo? Isn't this the complex heart of the matter? The text has glossed over this inconvenient lacuna in the time-honored fashion. As a result, the medical student may have the tough job of understanding and memorizing the diagram, but we have all been left with the far tougher task of reading the mute white space between the lines.

Imagine you're driving in a screw, and in the process the screwdriver slips and digs into the back of your hand. (The following description can be found, greatly amplified and in more scholarly detail, in *Immunology the Way You Always Wanted It to Be Taught*, by Dr. Edward Golub and Dr. Douglas Green.)

Immediately, the blood vessels in the area constrict, presumably to lessen damage and loss of blood, but almost at once the arteries dilate, bringing more blood to the area. But the blood—or, more specifically, the fluids and cells in the blood—can't do any good in the blood vessels themselves; they must get out into the surrounding tissues where the damage is, and where any bacteria that were on the tip of the screwdriver have been driven.

This is a job for the mast cell, which, like most players in the immune response, can be adapted for a variety of roles. Created in the bone marrow, mast cells take up lodging just beneath the skin like a garrison of sentries, and the impact of the screwdriver damages them, releasing their granular contents, as listed above. The histamine causes the cells that make up the wall of the blood vessel—the endothelial cells—to contract, and at once the fluid portion of the blood starts to leak out of the blood vessel into the tissue, causing swelling, also known as edema. This fluid has a number of antibacterial molecules in it; the healing process has already begun.

But this would be a small, local response. The immune system's job is to amplify the immediate, local antibacteriological activity and bring in whatever other agents are necessary. To do so, a series of events are set in motion that are called, with a degree of vividness and poetry rare in medical jargon, the inflammatory cascade. Most of our defensive molecules are biologically inert until notified of danger—to be otherwise would be like going to the office carrying a loaded gun with the safety off—so, like a waterfall, one set of molecules activates another to make two components, one of which steps up the process of vasodilation, the other converting a different molecule and making that split in two, each step activating other molecules that activate other molecules. Diagramed on paper, it looks exactly like a waterfall, or a fountain. One trickle of the cascade, for example, called *complement,* leads ultimately to the arrival of a large, complicated molecule with the Pentagonic name of the Membrane Attack Complex. The MAC forms on the surface of the invading bacteria, and as soon as another product of the cascade is added, the MAC is activated and drills holes in the membrane of the bacterium, killing it.

Even so, an entire division of the body's defenses has not yet arrived: the white blood cells.

Once again, the problem is one not of weaponry but of recruitment: the cells must be drawn to the affected area and enticed out of the bloodstream. This is more of a challenge than it would seem: the newly created gaps between the endothelial cells are large enough to let fluids escape, but not cells. If cells could escape from the blood vessels, vast amounts of internal bleeding would occur at every tiny injury. Moreover, cells, though remarkably complex, don't have minds of their own, and unless changes occur they will simply sweep past the injured area, bouncing off the walls of the blood vessels in what looks like a delightfully unconcerned fashion.

Whenever tissue is damaged, cytokines—messenger molecules, in effect—are released. At once they have a curious but vital effect on the endothelial cells in the nearby blood vessels: they force them to grow molecules that act like the hairs of Velcro. From now on, whenever a white blood cell called a neutrophil courses down the blood vessel, it will get snagged, and instead of bouncing off the wall, it will roll along it, becoming activated as it does so. Once again, the cascade of activation takes place, and as an end product, amazingly, the neutrophil comes to a complete stop, elongates itself, squeezes through the gap between the endothelial cells of the bloodstream wall, and slithers off through the damaged tissue, following a chemotactic scent trail like a bloodhound, in search of a foreign microbe to engulf and devour.

The next troops to arrive are the macrophages, whom we have already met. They, too, ingest bacteria, but they have two other functions: one (as we've seen) is to set in motion the long-term, specific immune response, which creates large numbers of T-cells and antibodies specific to the invader the macrophage has destroyed so that and the next time the virus turns up, it gets destroyed more quickly and efficiently. The other is to ingest the dead neutrophils and clean up the area so that the cytokines are no longer being released, the inflammatory cascade stops, the swelling goes down, and the area returns to normal.

The problem with asthma is that for some unknown reason, or possibly for several unknown reasons, the inflammatory response doesn't stop. As far as anyone can tell, even in those of us with mild asthma (and possibly even in people who have not yet noticed asthma symptoms) the airway tissues are heavily infiltrated with inflammatory cells (mast cells, basophils, eosinophils, neutrophils), whose presence has two effects: their very presence is a sign that something is amiss, and chemotactic messengers are sent out to attract other mediators to the area; and the antibacteriological substances they release, being highly toxic, cause local tissue damage. Eosinophils, for example, release a chemical called Major Basic Protein, which is powerful and nonselective enough to do extensive damage to our own cells—and this damage itself triggers more danger signals. Damage causes alarm that causes damage that causes alarm.

By now we are suffering a local but unmistakable autoimmune disaster. A harmless substance, misidentified, has turned us against ourselves. As Lewis Thomas wrote: "Our arsenals for fighting off bacteria are so powerful, and involve so many different defense mechanisms, that we are in more danger from them than from the invaders. . . . All this seems unnecessary, panic-driven . . . a response to propaganda. . . . We tear ourselves to pieces because of symbols, and we are more vulnerable to this than to any host of predators."

The cilia, the tiny hairs that catch and remove foreign particles, may flake away with the outermost layer of skin so the airway looks moth-eaten and has lost an important line of defense. In their place appear an unusual number of goblet cells, which produce a copious amount of mucus that itself is swarming with inflammatory cells, especially eosinophils.

A thicket of capillaries builds up in the airway wall, and a thick layer of collagen—scar tissue—develops beneath the epithelium as if misguided repair work were desperately taking place, the Highways Department pouring coat after coat of tar on the wrong highway. Meanwhile, chronic inflammation makes the airways sensitive to a wide variety of irritants—smoke, smog, exhaust, chemical fumes in the workplace, perfume—which may either simply stoke the inflammation or trigger an asthma attack, not so much because of an allergic response (though this may be the case) but simply because the airways are so sensitive.

The chronic-inflammation model sheds an interesting light on bronchoconstriction, too. Everyone's airway muscles constrict and relax to regulate our breathing—to prevent us from inhaling a massive jolt of frigid air, for example. It seems as if the bronchoconstriction in an asthmatic is no more extreme than in a normal person; it just happens at less provocation, and the airway itself is already so severely narrowed by the thickening of the walls and the amount of mucus present that the effect of a normal degree of constriction is to reduce air intake to dangerous levels. In this light, using a beta-agonist inhaler is merely crisis management rather than treatment of the deeper problem, and the medication or its propellant may in itself become an irritant. The treatment of choice is now cromolyn (which seems to inhibit both allergic and inflammatory activity) and steroids (which are anti-inflammatories). Even if we don't know what is causing this madness, if we can suppress the inflammatory activity, then we can at least limit the damage we're doing to ourselves.

As more and more cytokines—chemical messengers—are identified, it's tempting to see the entire problem as an Information Age issue: we've found the big, active, potent players; now we need to find and understand the minnows that suddenly seem all-important, conveying information (or, in this case, what seems to be misinformation) that can cause radical changes in the behavior of everyone around them. Everything seems complex and fluid; the extrinsic-intrinsic model seems hopelessly linear, insultingly reductive, like a binary calculator circa 1940, built of old telephone relays.

I wanted to write an accurate, interesting, comprehensible explanation of the process of chronic inflammation that was so vivid and so accurate that it would win not only a Nobel Prize for Science but a Nobel Prize for Literature as well, and get optioned as a screenplay. In the end, I failed. I failed for the basic reason that you can't describe what you don't understand.

Heaven knows, I tried. I went to lectures on asthma. I interviewed local, national, and international asthma specialists. I read books on allergy and immunology, and probably three dozen articles with titles like "New Insights into Airway Inflammation by Endobronchial Biopsy," and "Persistent and Latent Viral Infections in the Pathology of Asthma," and "Mechanisms of Hyperresponsiveness: Platelet-Activating Factor." I read a chapter of a book not yet published, and a chapter of a book not yet written.

I gave up not because some of the best minds in the medical world were baffled, though this is true, but because some of the other best minds in the medical world *had given up even asking the questions.* "Oh, I'm afraid I don't know anything about that," one expert said. "You should talk to my colleague X. She knows all about that stuff." And I realized that I had heard that same message more and more often as I'd plunged blindly on down the ever-narrowing, ever-branching airway of specialist research: whenever one reached a fundamental question about asthma, for the sake of one's sanity it was best not even to ask it.

So I struggled back out like a bruised cave explorer, clutching no gold but a fistful of questions I'd found down there in the passages so narrow that I could only reach down blindly with an outstretched arm:

• What causes some people to develop chronic inflammation? What exactly is happening in the bronchial wall, and what is in charge? What causes short-term inflammation to become long-term or chronic? What chemicals and cells are involved, and how do they give orders or carry information? What role do the nerves play? Is it possible that the various players in the immune system are all affected in some way by the mind?

• What else does IgE do, apart from triggering mast cells? Does it set in motion a vastly more complex and long-term immune response, or is it itself only part of that global response?

• If the mast cell and its histamine are so important in asthma, why is it that people with other diseases such as mastocytosis, who routinely have enormous amounts of histamine circulating in their bloodstream, have no breathing problems?

• Is the mast cell involved in airway dysfunction even without allergen exposure?

• Many of the abnormal cell activities seem to be taking place to some extent in people with allergies who have never had asthma symptoms. Does this mean that a pre-asthmatic condition exists, a low-grade inflammation that for some reason doesn't yet produce the characteristic hyperresponsiveness and wheeze of asthma? Is there a threshold at which point an irreversible change occurs and the dark miracle takes place?

• Is the chronic inflammation the result of a virus—perhaps one of the childhood respiratory viruses that often seem to be the precursor of asthma—that takes up permanent residence in the airways and provides a constant-enough supply of foreign protein to maintain a chronic inflammation?

• If asthma is an inflammatory condition, and corticosteroids are effective suppressors of inflammatory activity, why does some kind of underlying process return, sometimes with a vengeance, if we stop taking the steroids? And even if, after ten years on steroids, we've lost all signs of epithelial damage and unusual inflammatory activity, *how come we still wheeze?*

• Are mast cells involved in exercise-induced asthma, or not? If exercise-induced asthma is purely a function of cold or dry air, why does cromolyn help prevent it?

• Is the very idea of inflammation an anachronism, an absurdly crude term that fails to describe adequately a multitude of different immune activities?

Personally, I suspect that "asthma" will turn out to consist of (at least) two largely separate but overlapping diseases. One of them will be allergic in origin, characterized by a heavy release of mucus and running mostly in atopic families; this may not involve chronic inflammation at all, especially in people who only become asthmatic every five years when they accidentally eat peanuts, for example. The other will be a form of permanent airway damage, characterized by the dry wheeze of chronic inflammation. The second "asthma" will be found to be caused by a variety of shocks to the airways—environmental, occupational—including the cellular fallout of the first, for allergic activity is, confusingly, both short-lived and capable of wreaking longer-lasting damage: when I have a particularly vivid attack of hay fever, for instance, it almost always converts into a mild sinus infection. The first signs of allergic asthma, then, will be treated far more aggressively than at present, in the hope of driving a wedge between it and its more dangerous, longer-lived cousin.

Even though I can't tell you, despite all this mucking around at the cellular level, what causes asthma, in a sense

I've been privileged: I've seen something rarer than the bored certainties of the diagnosing M.D. and more vital than the expensive shibboleths of the consulting specialist. I have been down to the lowest galleries and seen the miners at work (mole-blind in the darkness, stumbling over each other, pointing in different directions and arguing) chipping away at the bedrock of ignorance.

Reading the medical journals, one would assume that these are the only questions worth asking about asthma, and that everything else should come to a halt while the experts carry out the white-coated, round-shouldered microscopic inquiry that we think of as the proper activity of medical science.

After a while, though, I began to realize that out in the large, dirty, complicated world where medical science is as naive and vulnerable as an Eagle Scout in the Bowery, there were nonmicroscopic questions to be asked—questions which implied that even if we find the "asthma gene" or the truant inflammatory mechanism, it will do us precious little good.

Patient Progress Report No. 2

MAY 1992—There must be a Latin prefix to go on the front of the word *pathology* (*peripathology,* perhaps?) to denote the process of re-redirection that takes place when medical treatment suppresses the symptoms of a basic disorder, making it crop up elsewhere, in a different form.

I sympathize with the homeopaths here: it's hard to treat a condition, they complain, that has been complicated and disguised, buried beneath successive strata of drugs and countersymptoms. No sooner had I gone on inhaled steroids and become miraculously symptom-free than I developed a mysterious and annoying sensation that something had got stuck in my throat and needed to be swallowed. When I swallowed, the sensation went away but, after perhaps ten seconds, returned, insisting to be dealt with. Eating or drinking made it last longer. X rays revealed nothing out of the ordinary—no lump in the tissue of the esophagus, no obstruction—and the only remedy was not to eat for five, six, as much as eight hours. It was maddening.

(Later I find myself wondering whether this was not a cousin of asthma, a disorder descended not from the tracheal line but from the esophageal, another clenched manifestation of tension.)

Only months later, when the semester was long over and my digestion had finally settled down, did it vanish; but within a couple of weeks it was replaced by an equally mysterious tension in my right forearm that began in the fingers and, if the situation provoked enough anxiety, spread all the way up to my shoulder. I took to driving my car sitting on my right hand; at one meeting I had to lay my arm across the chair back and, to concentrate on relaxing it, glower at it. Then the summer semester ended, and that oddity, too, disappeared.

All these micro-ailments cry out to me, like Othello, to find *the cause*. Are they just replacements for the tension headaches I used to get (because I now habitually do neck rolls and relax my neck when things get rough)? Has the tension had to go elsewhere?

Last week I met a renowned pharmacologist who specializes in asthma. I told him about mine. "Are the symptoms under control?" he demanded. "That's the goal, you know." But surely controlling symptoms is in a way the opposite of self-understanding, and sometimes if it isn't one thing, it'll be another. And the next might be cancer. In fact, it stands to reason that the more adept we get at knocking off symptoms we can control, the sooner we'll reach ones that we can't.

PART III

Know Your Enemy

Pet Theories

I soon found that there was no shortage of theories as to why asthma is on the increase.

The first held that in fact it isn't. Some doctors are skeptical of the figures, arguing that they simply show that a wider range of symptoms is now being diagnosed as asthma, such as what might previously have been called "bronchitis with wheezing," and that now more physicians are aware that a persistent cough may be a sign of asthma. But while there may or may not be more asthma, there's no doubt that serious asthma is more common. Hospitalization rates almost tripled between 1970 and 1980, while all other childhood diseases remained stable. All in all, the statistics suggest that doctors are taking asthma more seriously, and there is good reason to do so.

Every asthma specialist, it seems, has a different explanation. Some have the whiff of common sense about them; some have the gamier smell of pet notions or of professionally vested interests. It seems reasonable to look hard at the changing dynamics of the working family, for example. As more and more families need two incomes, the number of children spending several hours a day in day-care, preschool, or after-school programs has risen dramatically: a third of American three- to four-year-olds attend preschools or day-care centers, and in other countries the percentage is higher. As any parent with a child in day care knows, if one child has a cough or dripping nose, every child gets it. The more respiratory viruses a child contracts, especially at such a young age, the greater the risk of asthma. And it's not only viruses children bring to the play group or the school: a recent study in Sweden found higher levels of cat allergen in school classrooms than in some homes with a cat.

Those who believe that most asthma is caused by sensitization to dust mites have found plenty of evidence that our own notions of progress have been our downfall. For example: in the 1960s (in England, at least) the three new improvements that showed your home was the residence of a family of taste and substance were central heating, double glazing, and wall-to-wall carpeting. If the dust mite is as important a factor in asthma as its partisans believe, all three were health hazards. Central heating probably reduced mold but ensured that now dust mites could flourish all the year round. Double glazing and other "energy efficient" features of modern home construction not only sealed indoor pollution indoors, but tended to allow the humidity to rise, which dust mites appreciated. (Allergists nowadays warn against humidifiers, which also provide a fine sporing ground for molds.) And carpets, like stuffed furniture and mattresses, became the perfect haven for allergens. Cat allergen can linger in carpets and furniture for up to twenty-four weeks after a cat has been removed. A mattress can contain more than a hundred thousand dust mites; and the same number of mite fecal particles, which are equally potent allergens, can adhere to a gram of dust. A well-swept Shaker home would have harbored virtually no mites; nowadays, we unwittingly collect them as symbols of the home beautiful. Even our new energy-saving cold-water laundry detergents may work against us, as mites are killed at 130 degrees Fahrenheit, but not at 70 degrees.

The most vivid illustration of the connection between asthma and the comforts of Western civilization was provided by unfortunate highlanders of Papua New Guinea. In eight South Fore villages, the incidence of asthma has risen from virtually nil to over 7 percent within the last two decades. Researchers discovered that over that period the men of the villages had acquired blankets in which they wrapped themselves to sleep. The rest of the villagers' furnishings was so spartan that there was nowhere for mites to nest (it's not clear whether any mites even existed in the villages before the advent of modern bedding materials), but the blankets were ideal, and the insects promptly took up residence, snug as a bug, at densities of well over a thousand mites per gram of dust.

One doctor suggested that in the rise of asthma we were seeing the results of our meddling in the amoral eugenics of evolution. In theory, he said, those of us with defective genes tend to die before we reach breeding age, thus weeding the algae out of the gene pool. By working to keep unhealthy children and young adults alive, we're defeating the process of natural selection. It's hard to believe, though, that the number of saved asthmatics who would otherwise have died is so vast that we see the difference in one generation.

Another told me that the exercise boom was to

blame: guys who set themselves impossible physical goals and end up out of breath find it so hard to admit their failure that they blame their breathlessness on asthma, he said. "Soon Gucci and Calvin Klein will bring out designer inhalers."

Still another hypothesized that the world was simply becoming a more stressful place—a hard theory to evaluate, as it isn't clear how stress causes asthma in one person, let alone millions, and it's hard to believe that there is more stress now than, say, during World War II.

Frankly, I didn't buy most of these theories. Each might explain a few cases, but not a worldwide increase, and not a national 6 percent increase of deaths per year. It was becoming clear that the medical insiders, the specialists, the professionals, did not have the answers. Was it possible that an outsider, a generalist, an amateur might? The idea was appallingly presumptuous. It was so presumptuous, in fact, that I got out a legal pad and began to make lists.

Family Practice

Taking stock of my ignorance, I realized that I knew virtually nothing about asthma in young children, so I asked to sit in on a brown-bag seminar that Barbara Frankowski, assistant professor of pediatrics at the University of Vermont College of Medicine, was running for half a dozen pediatric residents. A specialist in pediatric asthma, she is a short, cheerful, capable woman with the unshakable demeanor of an elementary-school teacher who knows where every one of the art supplies is.

She had already explained to me that getting as far as a diagnosis of asthma in children is more of a palaver than I would have expected. All wheezing, especially in small children, is not asthma. Babies in particular can have bouts of bronchiolitis, a chest-cold thingummy caused by a respiratory system virus, that look and sound for all the world like an asthma episode, only with more mucus. In an odd way, cause and effect are reversed, and the pediatrician diagnoses by treatment: if the respiratory infection is treated and the wheezing stops, it wasn't asthma. Q.E.D. If there's a family history of allergies and especially of asthma, and if the child has two or three bouts of wheezing with colds, Barbara said, cautiously, then he *may* have a problem *for a while*.

For the pediatrician to start throwing the term *asthma* around, she said, is a risk. Asthma is a condition that the pediatrician wants the parents to take seriously—far more so than a cold, or even a bronchitis. To diagnose too soon may cause more trouble than it's worth. If the pediatrician starts talking about asthma after the child has had only one or two attacks, will the parents be sufficiently motivated to quit smoking? Will the parents start treating the child differently—overprotectively, resentfully, guiltily—after the child has been labeled asthmatic? Will the family insurance cover a home nebulizer? By these and other such oblique questions, we slide backward toward a diagnosis of asthma.

As the residents gathered and opened their lunch bags and Tupperware, Barbara produced a handout that on one page diagrammed the action of the mast cell—this was medical-student stuff, and everyone flipped right past it—and on the next three pages summarized the current pharmacology of pediatric asthma. The residents were clearly at home here: one pointed out a medication that wasn't included (the handout was eighteen months old, an entire generation in the life of modern asthma pharmaceuticals); another cited a drug in common use in Europe that is doing wonders but has yet to be approved by the FDA. (The consensus in the medical community is that all the important asthma drugs are developed in Europe, and then the FDA holds them up at the border, maintaining its own version of Ellis Island: they appear in the United States years later, with their names changed.) The group was full of youthful certainty, even arrogance. Medication is the stuff of right and wrong answers to be memorized, of tests taken and passed by students who have arrived here thanks to their ability to take and pass tests.

But medication for children with asthma is not merely the drugs themselves. Just as important is what the military calls the delivery systems: the inhalers for the older kids; the nebulizers for those too young to be able to squeeze the inhaler and breathe in at the same time; the spacers like toilet-roll-sized tubes with mouthpieces that slow down the mist of particles so the child can take them in in more than one breath; the peak-flow meters, which measure when an asthmatic's lung function is and isn't at its best; even stethoscopes, though frankly not many parents' ears are educated enough to be able to tell the steady sibilance of asthma from the bubbling gurgle of bronchitis. It's now becoming common to prescribe a peak flow meter in moderate and severe cases so the child starts to develop an awareness of the rise and fall of her own symptoms and a sense of how and when to use her medications. If nothing else, this may have the benefit of making everyone involved feel less at the mercy of unpredictable attacks—especially the asthmatic child, for whom anxiety can become virtually a disease entity in itself.

Knowing her enemy, Barbara had the residents try using the inhalers and the peak-flow meters. Her point was made straightaway: they couldn't coordinate the release and the inhalation, coughing and spluttering as the medication hit the back of their throats, and grimacing in distaste. Today's lesson: a pediatrician's job isn't finished when the diagnosis is accurate and the medication is prescribed. The missing link, as always, is getting the medication into the patient, a job that takes both dedication and conviction on the part of the parent. The pediatrician, then, is part physician, part teacher, part evangelist: her job is to inspire that conviction.

But the lesson had already hit its point of diminishing returns. The students passed around the peak flow meter to see who could hit the max, the less mechanically minded trying to figure out how the Intal Spinhaler fit together and how the little pins burst the capsules containing the medication; and nobody listened to Barbara for a good ten minutes as she tried to explain the parents' position and the importance of the pediatrician-parent relationship. They were all too absorbed in the technocopia of asthma, not yet mature enough to realize that the biggest problems are human problems. As Barbara told me later, they were still thinking in terms of "What's the right answer?" and "How do I cure this?" Their real lessons will be learned, over and over again, in frustration and anger at children who run screaming from their nebulizer or, more likely, parents who make five trips to the ER before they'll take asthma seriously.

A physician treats patients; a pediatrician treats families. (No wonder I kept thinking of Barbara as a schoolteacher.) Unless the parents understand the illness and the treatment, the child may not get better. The pediatrician is therefore also more likely to think in terms of environment modification and lifestyle change, and to see it as her job to make recommendations in no uncertain terms.

By now the group was getting beeper calls, and the bundt cake someone had donated was down to its last slice. We discussed skin testing, that stock-in-trade of the hard-core allergists. Not all children need skin tests, Barbara explained, because not all asthmas are allergic. In fact, their greatest value may be a rhetorical one: *they get the parents to take the asthma seriously.* The blotchy magic, the undeniable demonstration of cause and effect, does wonders for the pediatrician who knows that nothing short of such a miracle will persuade the family to buy feather-free pillows or get rid of the cat.

Even this is an uphill struggle. The content and workings of a household are a kind of solid metaphor for the family, an extrusion, perhaps, spun out of the souls of its inhabitants. Any domestic change, therefore, is a radical change. The changes recommended for a young child with severe asthma disrupt the entire family. One pulmonologist I spoke to said that he had never managed to persuade anyone to give up smoking, and had only once managed to get a cat evicted. John Updike, who suffered severe asthma partly as a result of allergy to cats, wrote, "How could we get rid of two such venerable members of our family, who from kittenhood on had enriched our conjoined lives with lessons in birth and murder, flirtatiousness and fortitude, who had endured and tamed a succession of bouncy puppies and brought us gifts of half-chewed field mice many a dewy morning?" If we are to take his account in *Self-Consciousness* at face value, Updike astonishingly concluded "it seemed easier to get rid of me," and left his family.

For Barbara, the future for pediatric asthma lies in education, that subject with which Americans have such a love-hate relationship. We do a worse job of teaching parents about asthma than about any other chronic and severe childhood illness, she said. Look at diabetes: if a child is diagnosed as diabetic, the entire family goes straight to the hospital and doesn't leave until (in theory, at least) they know what the disease is, how to administer the insulin, and what will happen if they don't. Many asthma specialists would like to see such aggressive treatment for even mild asthma; but asthma, which is far more common than diabetes, presents a much trickier exercise in education. Instead of one shot a day, the child may need three or four doses that, if a nebulizer is needed, require a parent to sit with child in her lap for up to a quarter of an hour. Instead of one medication, though, the pediatrician may have to prescribe two or three, and the sheer process of discovering which medication works best may take six or nine months, during which time the parents become convinced that the doctor is either (a) incompetent, or (b) using little Joey as a guinea pig for shady pharmacological experiments. Meanwhile, the asthma may go underground for days, weeks, or even months, making it hard to decide if a course of treatment is working or—this will occur to parents—necessary. "No parent is going to give a child chronic medication for something that happens every so often," Barbara said.

Diabetes is simpler: give the child insulin, or she will go into a coma and may die. It's harder to know when or if disaster will strike an asthmatic child. It's hard to educate, under these circumstances, this lack of clear and present danger; and of course the health-insurance companies demonstrate their usual don't-look-at-us attitude by refusing to reimburse physicians or patients for time spent on prevention or education. The American Lung Association of Vermont has set up free-of-charge whole-family asthma education days that Barbara and other local asthma specialists have run at the hospital, but the problem with such programs and asthma camps is that they take place at the inconvenience and often the expense of the patient.

For my money, the best model is an asthma club set up by Eileen Humphrey, the school nurse of a middle school on the outskirts of Oxford, England. The club meets weekly at 1 P.M.——the school principal, in a stunning display of good sense, considered the club important enough to allow it to take place during lesson time——and students monitor their own breathing using a peak-flow meter, get advice on cold weather, allergies, and physical education, learn how to use their inhalers properly, read leaflets and books, and watch videotapes. About 12 percent of the school population attends regularly; even nonasthmatics turn up. There have been no major asthma attacks in the school since the club was set up, whereas there had been three or four a year before the club was started. Children with asthma now take part in all school activities, and absenteeism is very low.

"The children use their inhalers sensibly," Humphrey wrote in *Nursing Times*; "overuse and misuse of inhalers has ceased. Before the club started, some children appeared to be using their inhalers constantly. There had also been instances of other children taking inhalers [from asthmatics] and spraying them until empty. Conversely, children who needed to use an inhaler had been reluctant to do so in front of others." One teacher admitted that he could now use his inhaler in the classroom without embarrassment because the children were so used to them.

This is a profound transformation. Illness is usually isolating, and isolation breeds ignorance, stigma, shame. Redefining illness as part of the normal curriculum is a radical, radiant change. Who among us, like the teacher, wouldn't benefit from such an education?

Patient Progress Report No. 3

JULY 1992—The imperative of chronic illness, that I will have to keep taking the inhaled steroids for the rest of my life, sounds like such an old fogy's concern: "Are you sure you've taken your pills, dear?" Sickness, like age, is so strongly equated with weakness. From a week after the attack I carried an epinephrine syringe and an albuterol inhaler *everywhere*. In winter it was easier: both lived in the inner pocket of my flying jacket, and I could forget about them. In summer they were more obvious, rattling around in the pocket of shorts or shirt. It was inconvenient and awkward, but more importantly, I was ashamed. Luckily, my birthday is in June, and my girlfriend Barbara got me a real leather overnight bag and a black washing-tackle bag—"for all your pharmaceuticals," she said sarcastically. I started carrying it everywhere, like the slim personal cases French Canadians carry in Montreal. It was great: it also held my date book, my checkbook, my favorite fountain pen. For the first time I realized why women carry handbags. It was *having it all with you*; it was like traveling in a VW bus. After a while Barbara took to leaving her diaphragm case in it, and from then on the sense of shame was virtually gone.

PART IV

Doctor's Orders

Failure to Comply

The more asthma books for the layperson I read, the more I was struck by an odd tone that cropped up now and then in all of them, a strange combination of urgency and helplessness, a hollow echo beyond the solid wall of advice. Whenever the physician tried to emphasize the importance of following his prescribed course of action and medication, a suppressed frustration seemed to smoke through the lines as though he were trying to reach through the parallel bars of his measured, professional prose to grasp my throat, to yell, *This is the information that could save your life! Do you understand? Are you listening to me?*

After a while I realized that to the physician-author, his plump and well-intentioned book, the fruit of several years' work, in all likelihood represents the limits of what he can do outside his office: beyond the book is the patient suffering from a relatively easily controlled condition who will simply *not*—I imagine the author clenching his fists, knuckling his forehead, throwing his head back, taking a deep breath, relaxing his muscles with an effort of will—who will not follow doctor's orders, who seems (and I'm quoting, now) stubborn, aloof, clinging, bone-headed. The asthma patient is walking wounded; we are beyond the doctor's care or control, a test of the boundaries of his authority and of his ability to convince, to extend conviction beyond dominion.

"It's a rule of thumb," one doctor told me, "that if I see a hundred patients in my office, and I write them all out prescriptions and put them, there and then, right into their hands, twenty-five will never even have the prescription filled, twenty-five will have it filled but will take their medication three times or less, twenty-five will use it more than three times but will not follow the dosage, and only twenty-five will actually follow the dosage I've prescribed." (Other doctors I've spoken to regard this as an optimistic estimate.)

The same frustration was also turning up in the medical journals, the bulletin boards of professional gossip, where it had a name that evoked a bewildered and angry shaking of heads: patient noncompliance. Understanding the activity of L4 leukotrienes, it seemed, was a piece of cake compared to understanding the behavior of the patient on the street, out of the office, off the examining table. Which affects the whole equation, of course: if you don't know whether the patient is even taking the drug, you have no means of knowing if it is effective. Pandemonium was running through the asthma trenches, and with such complete failure in answering even the simple, hard-science questions, nobody seemed to know the answer to the difficult, social-science one: why people so uniformly fail to act in their own apparent self-interest.

The answers suggested by the professional literature left me grinding my teeth in fury. Intent on blaming the patient for behavior that they can't understand, the researchers seemed to have no sense that *the way in which asthma* (and illness in general) *is typically managed might be to some degree responsible for the problem.*

Let's take a typical example: an article in *Annals of Allergy* that studies ten patients with potentially fatal asthma who have not followed their doctors' orders. The authors find that in every case, even cases involving mental illness, the noncompliance is the patient's fault. A forty-year-old woman is criticized for being "unable to comprehend the importance of a defined and continuous medical regimen" because of "inadequate intellectual ability." Whose fault is this? If she has been given a health regimen that she can't understand, she hasn't been given a health regimen. An adolescent girl is likewise blamed for not understanding why inhaled steroids are important, and when she admits to heavy cigarette smoking she is dismissed as suffering from "adolescent noncompliance." (Teenagers, not surprisingly, are notoriously unlikely to comply, having escaped their parents' Compliance Patrol but not yet having learned a healthy instinct for self-preservation, and figure highly in the morbidity and mortality figures. We also have our own pressing emotional agenda: I was prescribed cromolyn at fourteen but never used it, being convinced that everyone would hear the whirring noise of the little plastic propellor in the dispenser and would make fun of me. I convinced my mother that I'd tried it and it hadn't worked. Two decades later I tried cromolyn again and it did a certain amount of good. Who knows what would have happened if I'd stuck with it as a teenager?)

The authors' most incredible conclusion follows the case history of an adolescent boy who had had no fewer than sixteen potentially fatal attacks in five years, and periodically discontinued his prednisone because he had been told by two physicians that prednisone would interfere with his growth. The authors' diagnosis: "prednisophobia." *What??* If finding fault is indeed a useful activity in such a case, it is surely not the boy who is to blame but, first, the state of our pharmacology, which leaves us relying on medications that have such serious potential side effects, and, second, the two doctors who "took this position although they had been informed the boy could die without maintenance prednisone." A fairer conclusion here would be "professional malpractice," but medical journals don't tend to throw that kind of language around. There is a happy outcome, of sorts: the authors report condescendingly that "with maturation" the boy is now taking his medicine and has remained well. No kidding. It would take a certain amount of maturation to survive such a ghastly series of asthma crises; it would take a hell of a lot more to survive being blamed for them, especially when the medical establishment is giving you potentially lethal advice. (The phrase "take one's medicine," meanwhile, continues to mean "accept punishment.")

Elsewhere, an eighty-year-old woman, who had been hospitalized twenty times (with four intensive-care-unit admissions for asthma) over a short period of time, had apparently suffered mainly from her previous physicians' failure to recognize the severity of her illness. Once again, the conclusion says nothing about professional incompetence. Instead, the authors point out that she also had cardiac disease and hypertension, both requiring medication, and that the result was "a somewhat confused geriatric patient." Their conclusion in this case: "geriatric overload." "Factors contributing to such overload might include multiple medications, depression or age-induced intellectual decline or confusion."

At this point I was seeing red. One of the most respected and highly honored doctors of my acquaintance, Dr. Stanley Burns, attributes his renowned ability to understand and care for patients to the fact that he himself has been seriously ill—in fact, he endured a long struggle with tuberculosis even before he qualified as a doctor. I wish the learned authors of this article could be hurled in and out of intensive care twenty times apiece and could find themselves talked to in language they barely understood and given treatments they could barely follow involving medications whose names were in Latin, so that they might discover whether even they, at their doubtless relatively youthful ages, didn't still suffer a little intellectual decline or confusion.

In any case, this tendency to regard noncompliance as aberrant and self-destructive behavior ignores the fact that *virtually no one I have interviewed follows his or her doctor's instructions routinely.* This is a worm in the heart of the entire medical process: for all the vast and expensive research spent on developing drugs and the time and money spent training doctors, very little is known about how we think of medicine and how we react to doctors. In fact, one obvious reason why people as a whole are getting no better despite the wonder drugs is that we are either not using the wonder drugs properly, or not using them at all.

Cabinet Reshuffle

M y informal research suggests that the most common reason why people don't take their medicine
is that they don't trust drugs. In my own case, I had a
wary and resentful dependence on the albuterol inhaler;
on the other hand, I was profoundly grateful for the inhaled steroids, yet already I was trying (against the allergist's advice) to wean myself from them, trying smaller
and smaller doses to see how little I could get away with. I
didn't realize how complex and contradictory my own attitudes were until I looked inside my bathroom medicine
cabinet.

The cabinet, I realized, was a showcase of ambiva-
lence towards medication, with a dozen containers of pills
at varying stages of plenitude. Three of the containers,
one of which was some five years old and therefore possibly either toxic or utterly inert, contained pills whose
usual weird techno-Latinate names no longer meant anything to me. Two contained the remains of courses of different antibiotics that I had given up on as soon as I started
feeling better, even though I've repeatedly been told that
one should take the entire course. One relatively recent

one was an almost-complete course of an antibiotic that Barbara had never used but might come in handy next time I had bronchitis. One was a painkiller I'd been given after knee surgery; I mistrusted it deeply, suspecting it of having caused mood swings and depression, but who knew when I might need a powerful painkiller again? One was Guiatex, which had apparently been prescribed only twelve weeks previously but already failed to ring a bell and wasn't even in the *Physicians' Desk Reference*; still, anything that recent was probably worth keeping. One was theophylline, which I had been prescribed during an attack of bronchitis-plus-acute-asthma, took for three days, and refuse to take now that I know a little about it. One was a fat tub of Seldane, which will come in handy next hay fever season. Overcome by confusion and shame, I sorted through them and threw four containers out—and then immediately retrieved them from the garbage, as I remembered hearing once that we are supposed to return unused prescriptions to the pharmacy, so that the containers can be used again and the landfills don't fill up with potent pharmaceuticals slowly leaching into the streams and making the trout glow.

Wait a minute, I thought. There's almost something tattily religious about this, a Virgin-Mary-in-a-bathtub above the bathtub, a display of half-swallowed faith in miracle drugs. This is not the same as hoarding half-empty cans of paint in case I'll ever need a quarter-pint of Ivory Satin or Tropical Manganese. These pills are potentially dangerous, yet I haven't disposed of them; they're potentially beneficial enough for me to squirrel them away, yet I didn't take them when I had the chance, despite having been told several times by reputable physicians that these pills are safe, necessary, and in most cases should be taken until they are all gone; and they certainly should not be hoarded for half a decade. One of them, some kind of enzyme that I think I bought from a chiropractor as a nutrition supplement that would speed up a tissue-healing process, wasn't sealed anymore and, when I examined the label more closely, didn't claim to have any USRDA values or even to help cure anything. I flung it into the wastebasket in a fit of 55 percent annoyance, 40 percent guilt plus trace elements of regret and frustrated intellectual curiosity.

And then, after a few moments' reflection, a little anger, too. What the hell am I supposed to make of a label that says nothing but "TAKE 1 TABLET BY MOUTH EVERY 12 HOURS GUIATEX LA S RGY-IN"? Is it really surprising that, according to the *Cambridge Encyclopedia of Language,* one pharmaceutical survey found that 33 percent of patients misunderstood the instruction "use sparingly," and "take two tablets four hourly" was interpreted in a variety of ways, including to mean "take eight tablets an hour"? Quite apart from their mannered and Latinate prose, the labels on prescription drugs follow the time-honored traditions of giving the patient absolutely nothing except orders: no warnings against combining this with other drugs, no warnings about possible side effects, no general content information of the kind we demand even of a packet of cornflakes, for God's sake, no information suggesting how to modify the dosage under certain conditions, no expiration date—not even a name that makes any sense. An FDA spokesperson informed me that until recently it was considered professional malpractice for the pharmacist even to discuss the drugs she was dispensing. Nowadays the pharmacist's role is becoming more active—partly because, unlike the doctor, she doesn't charge for advice—and I am handed more complete dosage instructions on a printed slip when I pick up my prescription; but these are still orders rather than explanations, and because they come separate from the medication, they are easily disconnected and lost.

The pharmacist is not the only party in a position to provide us with useful and enlightening information about these pharmacologically active substances we are about to ingest. After I'd been taking the inhaled steroids for about six months, I picked up a refill and found myself idly looking at the little folded paper slip inside the box. What struck me as odd straightaway was that by far the most noticeable instruction was to the pharmacist to detach the top five-sixths of the slip, keep it, and give the rest to the patient. Well, this makes a certain amount of sense, I thought: the pharmacist is supposed to keep this and cross-reference it with any other drugs we're taking and otherwise use her professional knowledge to protect her clients. My pharmacist dismissed this notion with a laugh. "No, we're just supposed to throw it away," he said.

The slip made very strange reading. The small part the patient was supposed to get included eight-step instructions on how to use the inhaler, and warnings to use it as prescribed, not to confuse it with other medication, not to throw the inhaler on the fire, and so on, all in type so small that thirteen lines take up a vertical inch. I could read it, but then I can also read the condensed version of the *Oxford English Dictionary* without the little magnifying glass that comes with it; heaven help most other people.

The part the pharmacist was supposed to detach and throw away was perhaps ten times as long. Some, admittedly, I didn't mind not knowing, consisting as it did of what I assume is bedtime reading for pharmacists—to wit: "Description: Beclomethasone diproprionate, USP, the active component of VANCERIL inhaler, is an anti-inflammatory steroid having the chemical name 9-Chloro-11 beta,17,21-trihydroxy-16 beta-methylpregna-1,4-diene-3,20-dione 17,21-dipropionate." This was followed by a diagram, presumably for pharmacists who are visually rather than verbally oriented, a diagram replete with hexagons, squashed hexagons, unfinished hexagons and little houses, all surrounded by phrases like $CH_2OCOC_2H_5$, which happens to be exactly the noise an asthmatic makes when she coughs.

The clinical pharmacology section told me that the drug has little or no untoward effect on rats, that it remains relatively localized and is principally excreted through the feces, but comes to the rather alarming conclusion that "the precise mechanism of the aerosolized drug's action in the lung is also unknown."

A little further down, under "Warnings," things got rather tense. "Particular care is needed in patients who are transferred from systemically active corticosteroids to Vanceril inhaler because *deaths due to adrenal insufficiency have occurred in asthmatic patients during and after transfer from systemic corticosteroids to aerosol beclomethasone diproprionate.*" At this point I took a deep breath and sat down for a while. Had I been one of many patients on generalized steroids, my doctor would of course have warned me about this, wouldn't he?

Further down, not even in the box marked "Warnings," is the sobering information that the long-term effects of the agent on humans are unknown, in particular its effects on developmental or immunologic processes in the mouth, pharynx, trachea, and lung.

What infuriates me is not so much that the inhaled steroids might contain potential dangers that nobody told me about; much of my alarm, I'm sure, arises from ignorance. Nor is it that I had just caught a glimpse of the clandestine relationship between physician and drugmaker, the calculations of danger and the admissions of ignorance that the doctor then typically hides behind the reassuring bedside—sorry, *office*side—manner. (Only one doctor's visit in five hundred is now a home visit.)

It's this: when I called the FDA and asked them to explain the logic behind this slip, which they identified as a Physician Package Insert, three different spokespeople gave me three different responses. All agreed that the drug company was required by law to print up the PPI, whose information was directed at the only party not involved in the exchange: the doctor. When I suggested that this was a waste of paper and a waste of a great opportunity to create a more informed patient, the first spokesperson told me, as my jaw bounced gently against my chest, that it was a legal requirement that the PPI be written in language that the public can*not* understand, presumably following the belief in the medical profession that what the patient doesn't know won't kill him, whereas what he does know might confuse and frighten him so much he'll go gray with worry or throw himself under a bus. When my research assistant called back to verify this astonishing information, a different spokesperson retorted that this was utter nonsense—and in any case the language in the PPI was perfectly comprehensible to the lay person. What? "9-Chloro-11 beta, 17, 21-trihydroxy-16 beta-methylpregna-1, 4-diene-3, 20-dione 17, 21-dipropionate"? I called back and got a third spokesperson, who sensibly said that no, of course the PPI was written for the physician; the FDA had tried to back legislation that would have compelled the drug companies to write package inserts for the patient instead of the doctor, but Ronald Reagan had vetoed this legislation as his first act in office. I called the FDA's legislative office to verify *that,* but nobody could; the relevant documents appeared to have been discarded, like the FDA's patient-friendly initiative and a billion PPIs.

Is it any wonder that we patients behave in an uninformed and erratic manner when, given the chance to inform us, the FDA compels the drug companies to publish information that explicitly keeps us in the dark and then gets thrown away without anyone's seeing it?

The jumble in my bathroom cabinet illustrates my pharmaceutical dilemma, and that of probably millions of other patients. The hoarding impulse shows just how emotionally and fiscally valuable drugs are and how rapidly we feel we might need them: it is, after all, a slow, awkward, and sometimes expensive process to go from symptom to relief via a doctor's appointment. (It also shows what fools we are if we instinctively believe that medicines are as simple and as transferable as cans of paint and that we can not only diagnose but prescribe for our-selves.) At the same time, we avoid taking drugs if at all possible. We may need them, but we don't trust them.

Twenty Percent Forever

Another reason I mistrust drugs is that it is virtually impossible to have faith in the people who make them. In fact, the more I learned about drug companies, the more my customary alert skepticism turned into outrage and open hostility at attitudes toward the sick that are at best cynical and at worst predatory.

First of all—and perhaps above all—pharmaceutical companies profit from the inevitable fact of human suffering. This in itself is surely immoral; but U.S. drug companies have been allowed to derive more profit from this captive market than their counterparts elsewhere in the world and even more than other manufacturing industries in the United States.

A drug company gouges a patient like a surgeon using a backhoe. U.S. drug companies ran an estimated $975 million trade surplus in 1992. Identical drugs available in the United States and Canada cost 32 percent more in the United States. The industry's average profit margin is four times the average for all companies in the Standard & Poor's index. Meanwhile, drug costs are the fastest-growing part of the health-care sector. Between 1985 and 1991 prices for prescription drugs rose by 67 percent, two and a half times the inflation rate.

Companies making asthma drugs are especially profitable. In May 1991 the *Financial Times* announced that Schering-Plough was "advancing boldly" in the worldwide pharmaceutical marketplace, according to the company's annual report. In fiscal 1990 net income amounted to $565 million, up 20 percent from the previous year, with pharmaceutical sales increasing by 17 percent to reach $2.6 billion. The company's biggest sales category was asthma and allergy, in which it has Proventil (salbutamol) registering 1990 sales of $315 million (up by 22 percent), Theo-Dur (sustained-release theophylline), again selling over $100 million, and Claritin (loratidine), achieving sales of over $70 million in its second full year on the market.

An enormous portion of those profits are spent not on developing new drugs or wading through the red tape necessary to have them approved by the FDA, but on promotion, advertising, and marketing. Dr. Stephen Schondelmeyer, professor of pharmaceutical economics at the University of Minnesota, has estimated that the average drug company spends 20 percent of its budget on promotion—*ten times as much as most consumer-based industries.*

The drug companies are also not above trying to mislead doctors. You'd imagine that in the professional periodicals, at least, drug companies would be kept to the straight and narrow, but a 1992 UCLA study of 109 ads in ten leading medical journals found that 100 contained "deficiencies in areas for which the FDA has established explicit standards for quality." Forty percent of the ads reviewed exaggerated a drug's benefits or downplayed its known hazards; 30 percent cited statistics from "inconclusive, dissimilar, or poorly designed studies"; and 30 percent included misleading graphs or tables. If these are the ads directed at those most likely to spot their errors or liberties with the truth, what chance does that leave the muddled layperson, who is still at the kindergarten level of trying to spell "relief"?

It leaves us watching television news, but there too the drug companies have exerted their influence. A notorious example is the Billie Bloom videotape, which looked like a locally produced spot in the evening news report on KGTV in San Diego in early 1987, but it was actually a "video news release," produced by a public-relations agency in New York, nominally on behalf of the Asthma and Allergy Foundation of America but paid for by Key Pharmaceuticals, a contributor to the foundation and maker of a drug that got a favorable mention in the tape. Billie Bloom, an eleven-year-old asthmatic, reenacted on camera an asthma attack that occurred after she had switched medicines. The thrust of the videotape was that generic drugs can be less safe than brand-name ones—a message that the FDA considered misleading, but on which it took no action. In all, *The New York Times* reported, the tape was aired thirty-one times by KGTV and twenty-two other stations and was seen by an estimated 1.3 million people.

Print advertising and video news releases represent only a small part of most drug companies' marketing budgets. In 1988, for example, Key Pharmaceuticals, spending some of the profits from its theophylline-based asthma medications, invited three hundred physicians for a three-hour dinner aboard a luxury yacht in Newport Harbor,

California, to pitch them the company's new heart drugs. Drug companies also pass out free pens, notepads, calendars, and other miscellaneous office supplies by the ton. Ask a doctor to write you a quick note and nine times out of ten it'll come on notepad paper with a heading like "Thanaxatol: superior post-fibrillative recuperation" in exciting, bold, maroon letters.

Of course, drug companies also underwrite perfectly legitimate scientific conferences, thereby not only creating a degree of dependence but also muddying the ethical waters thoroughly.

While writing this book, I stumbled on the sad case of Jennifer Pollock, whose premature birth in 1983 resulted in a respiratory condition for which she was prescribed Somophyllin Oral Liquid, a brand of theophylline derivative manufactured by Fisons. Three years later, she developed a viral illness and began having difficulty breathing. Her doctor increased the dosage. Theophylline "dumping" took place, the amount of theophylline in the blood jumped rapidly to toxic levels, and two days later, Jennifer suddenly developed seizures that resulted in permanent injuries, including brain damage.

During the legal proceedings that followed, it emerged that for several years Fisons had been informing a select group of some two thousand specialists referred to as KIPs, or Key Influential Physicians, of studies that reported some of the dangerous side effects of Somophyllin. Those selected physicians were doctors whom Fisons had targeted as potential customers for Intal, a patented Fisons asthma medication based on cromolyn sodium. Dozens of Intal marketing memos and letters read out in court highlighted the dangers of theophylline.

At the same time, however, the company was still selling theophylline products, mysteriously failing to mention any of these alarming studies or the dangers they revealed.

Doctor's Orders

W hen I first plowed through the medical library's files on compliance, which suggested that asthma patients were among the worst offenders, with noncompliance rates approaching 90 percent, I unthinkingly nodded along with the often-unstated assumptions of the researchers: that patients who didn't follow the medical regimens set out for them were stupid or self-destructive. Who but a fool turns down offers of help and good advice?

I continued in this state of comfortable mild bigotry for about three weeks before I realized with a shock that I, for all my pious intentions and Oxford education, was no more obedient a patient than most of these offenders. I remembered with a dull shock that the specialist I saw after my November attack had given me a prescription for inhaled steroids, with some dosage instructions orally and in writing, and told me to come back once in a few weeks, again in April or May, at the beginning of the pollen season, and again in a year's time. I didn't go back for the next appointment; I went back several months later and then skipped the spring appointment and the one-year follow-up completely.

I didn't go back because I didn't like him. He is widely respected as a physician who keeps up with the latest research and is prepared to champion a treatment, no matter how unfashionable, if good evidence supports it, but he struck me as condescending, aloof, even sneering. He was good enough to take extra time to answer my questions, even to send me extra information by mail, and I know I should overlook his personal manner out of gratitude, let alone self-interest; but instead he set in motion the complex internal dialogue that bedevils all of us patients who withhold our trust: Is he peddling his own pet theories? Does he really know what he's talking about? Is he prescribing this just to keep me quiet? Doesn't that dosage sound rather high?

Even this litany of uncertainty, though, is just a rationalization for something more powerful but less easy to admit. I didn't set up the second appointment because in some elemental, childish way I wanted him to be as concerned about my illness as I was; I wanted him to be my protector. *If you have another attack as serious as this one,* he instructed me, *you must see me at once;* but as I was enfolding myself gratefully into the wings of his concern, he added, *during office hours on the next working day.* From his point of view, this was perfectly rational: the E.R. is far better equipped to deal with an attack of asthmatic anaphylaxis than a suburban specialist's office. To his credit, he would have been prepared to give me help and advice outside office hours—in fact, if I'd stopped to think about it, I'd have remembered that in the past he had done so, for me and others I know. But illness is not a rational experience: I wanted him to be there with me when I was at my worst, so he could see my symptoms firsthand, so I could feel that he was down in the asthma trenches with me, getting his feet as muddy as mine. ("Most doctors want the allergic patient to go somewhere else," another allergist told me. "They frighten [the doctors]. Doctors like diseases they can cure. They don't like people like that in their offices, staggering in, blue in the face—it disrupts the office routine.")

To hell with that. When six or eight weeks went by and no receptionist called to jog my memory about the next appointment, I was convinced that he didn't care. He was a specialist with a full waiting room, I thought, stoking my resentment against him; he must make five times my annual salary, yet the sign in the front office still demanded payment in full at the time of each visit. Fuck him. (I conveniently forgot that he does pro bono work each year, and that he had allowed me and others to pay bills late.) When I did return it was to prove him wrong. He had said that I was probably suffering permanently reduced lung function, by implication because I hadn't come to see him sooner; when I went back, not having wheezed for four months, I blew so hard into the peak-flow meter the needle hit the top of the chart. Take that.

He had done his best, but instead of getting me to follow the precise duplicated instructions he had handed me, he had pushed me—to be more accurate, I had retreated—into the shadows of medicine; and since then I've discovered that virtually every asthmatic I've interviewed who has seen him has also done a bunk, preferring to see a physician they like and trust, even if he or she is less of an expert.

We all have our reasons for mistrusting doctors. In some cases we expect them to perform miracles and they can't; in other cases someone we love suffers and dies and we convert our helplessness into anger at those we feel should have done more, and disguise our grief, too, as anger.

The fact is, simply being unwell creates a deep and largely unpredictable emotional turbulence; visiting the doctor stirs things up immeasurably more. One day someone will carry out a study that will show that patients only *hear* 30 percent of what their physician says, let alone understand and remember it. The encounter in the doctor's office—no longer in the home—may be a routine, even tedious, one for the physician, but for the patient it is fraught with complex issues, any of which may be more emotionally compelling than what the doctor is saying. To put it bluntly, the doctor is not the one being asked to drop his pants and have a lubricated finger inserted up the rectum. As the patient leaves, the doctor's command *Be sure you follow the dosage exactly* echoes emptily, like the prison warden saying *Keep out of trouble, now* as the gates close behind the convict who's been waiting for five years for someone to give him a command he doesn't have to obey.

One doctor told me the story of a patient who wrote down in note form and diagrams everything that he said to her, and he assumed that she therefore understood and would remember it all perfectly. Not at all: her note taking was actually a way of not listening or taking in what he was saying, because she was so afraid of what it might mean. By writing it all down, she was diverting the information around her brain and onto the paper; when she got home, she was free to interpret whatever she had written down however she liked.

This highly unequal power relationship can't help but set off still more complex reactions leading generally in the direction of either resentment or dependence. My own experience with the allergy specialist illustrated the resentment; in *Late Night Thoughts on Listening to Mahler's Ninth Symphony,* Lewis Thomas, suffering from serious cardiac arrhythmia requiring a pacemaker, illustrates how we can gravitate toward dependence and away from alert participation: "I would have thought that as a reasonably intelligent doctor-patient I would be filled with intelligent, penetrating questions, insisting on comprehending each step in the procedure, making my own decisions, even calling the shots. Not a bit of it. I turn out to be the kind of patient who doesn't want to have things explained, only to have things looked after by the real professionals."

It's even possible to have both attitudes at once. One remarkable study asked a group of asthma patients, all volunteers, to try using a new inhaler a specified number of times a day. They were told that at the end of the study the inhaler would be weighed to make sure the appropriate amount of medication had been expelled. What they weren't told was that the inhaler contained a computer chip that recorded *when* each spray took place. When the asthmatics returned their inhalers, the researchers discovered that 14 percent of them had "dumped" their medication the day before the study ended, shooting off virtually the entire contents so that the inhaler would weigh the "right" amount and they would therefore "please" the physicians. (This is not so odd; it's the asthma equivalent of flossing frantically for two days before the appointment with the dentist.)

Pleasing the doctor is an old habit. Typically, doctors have taken on a paternal, almost a moral responsibility for the patient, and have tried to achieve compliance rather like drill sergeants by using clear information and the voice of authority. "I cannot rise out of my bed till the physician enable me," wrote John Donne, "nay, I cannot tell that I am able to rise till he tells me so." The phrase "doctor's orders" has not found a permanent place in the language by accident.

But this process of diagnosis and prescription assumes a static system, in which the participants—doctor, illness, patient, drug—are known and unchanging. In fact, the relationship is extremely fluid. The sheer fact that the patient can think is enough to throw off all the best-laid regimens. Let's follow one simple sequence.

When I was prescribed the inhaled steroids I was supposed to take them four times a day, two puffs at a time, but immediately it began to vary, partly by accident, partly by intent. Sometimes I just forgot; the fear of death had receded, and the fear of missing a deadline started to seem more urgent—not to mention more likely. Just as we metabolize our medication, breaking it down, making use of it over a period of time, *we also metabolize information.* The doctor's order comes out as cogent and direct as a column of smoke rising from a cigarette; but after a time that is impossible to calculate it wavers, then breaks up, eddying in all directions. After a month without asthma—without the symptoms of asthma, I should say—I started wondering if I could get by on three doses a day. Steroids are, after all, serious stuff. The makers of

Vanceril admit that long-term effects of the drug, or the propellant, are unknown. Better to take as little as possible, I thought.

Noncompliance can also mean overuse of medication, especially in a disease as terrifying as severe asthma: we can easily develop an overwhelming emotional attachment to a drug that we think will help us breathe. Some asthmatics have inhalers littered all over the house—not so much because they won't be able to walk ten yards to find one, but because the notion of not being near one is so unsettling. Others use their albuterol not every four hours, as recommended, but as often as every twenty minutes, which causes heart flutters, a constant mild anxiety, and still further dependence on the inhaler.

Moreover, some noncompliance is probably a healthy sign. Colloquially, primary-care physicians estimate that perhaps a third of their patients have no serious organic disease and may simply want someone to talk to, in which case an unfilled prescription may be a sign that the patient is aware of the therapeutic value of conversation.

In the last few years the power relationship between doctor and patient has come under challenge, and every so often lip service is paid to the notion of making the patient responsible for his or her treatment, but this is a disturbingly new idea to both patient and doctor. One author on asthma, for example, had clearly been to a conference in which some radical theorist had proposed that the patient be enlisted as a member of the health-care management team, and he put this idea to the reader-patient. "You are part of the asthma management team," he proclaimed. Unfortunately, it was clear that certain aspects of this novel egalitarian notion had escaped him, as he went on to stress a role that involved *loss* of involvement, status, and responsibility.

"As important as it is for the doctor to correctly assess the medication needs of the patient [what, no other needs apart from that?], it is equally important for the patient to realize that he or she is an important part of the management team." This sounds respectful enough; but what does that important activity consist of? "If you tend to downplay your asthma and to take prescribed medications randomly rather than as directed, discuss this with your doctor." The patient's important role, then, is to fess up when he hasn't done what he was told. "In addition, if you panic and become frightened when your asthma flares, your doctor must know this."

Wait a moment: what is the *positive* role for the patient? To be informed? To be in charge of his own treatment, with the doctor as a professional adviser, like a tennis coach? And shouldn't this agreement go both ways? Shouldn't the doctor be taking home a little form that says something like "If I play a round of golf instead of reading the latest *Journal of Asthma,* I will discuss this with my patient," or "If I become angry and defensive when the patient asks me to make a house call during a bad attack, I should apologize"? How the hell do you expect the patient to come forward and admit fear, guilt, uncertainty, or ignorance if the doctor behaves like a tyrant with a flair for occasional condescension?

Asthma causes noncompliance not because we are congenitally stupid or stubborn, but because severe asthma causes a double rejection of reason. In the throes of suffocation we don't want a cool medical intervention, we want someone to cling to in abject terror. (Lacking a doctor, I had called "Help me. Help me" to a fireman, who had been as helpless as I.) "Asthma is such a frightening disease," said Tim Thompson, one of the few doctors I've met who understands the needs of the asthmatic, "that an asthmatic wants someone to bond to." As soon as he said "bond," I vividly imagined the doctor I'd never had, a knowledgeable friend, present and comforting: I saw myself bent over, gripping his arm, trying to breathe, knowing that he could be trusted, and that I could allow myself to be seen in this moment of panic and weakness.

Which is, of course, the second rejection of reason. Once the attack is over—which may, after all, be only a few minutes later—the disease seems to vanish, and we are left feeling not only scared to the core, but also very foolish. It's as if a tidal wave had crashed through our bedroom window in Kansas, overwhelming us, taking us to the point of drowning, and then had withdrawn, leaving no mud on the carpet, no damp clinging to the bedclothes. How can we not be ashamed of our panic, our moment of weakness—especially we men, perhaps? This makes it all the harder to see a doctor, when we have no symptoms to justify our poaching of his time, only an emotional residue that is all the more uncomfortable for having no cause that we can show. His cool professional manner rebukes our desire to blurt out, "Doctor, I'm scared," and his trained reply, "What seems to be the trouble?" reminds us that this is supposed to be an intelligent exchange of medical information. Frankly, he would rather we cope with our fear on our own: this kind of medical intercourse is in danger of being too entangled, too sticky for his liking. So he dismisses us and we beg for something more, or else our pride tells us we'd rather go with the patent medicines and try to suppress the anxiety, though to do so will lead us to be accused of denial. All medicine is driven and distorted by fear; asthmatics are merely an extreme case because the condition is so common, so frightening, and so quickly over. Or maybe the ideal of cool professional detachment is simply the wrong model. It may be a sign of my own weakness or immaturity, but there have been many times in my life when there was nothing I wanted more than a doctor to bond to.

In the end, compliance is an issue that extends beyond asthma to every stage of illness and health. What about the invisible noncompliers, those who will never visit a doctor for any illness because for them to be ill is to be weak, and ashamed of that weakness, and consequently angry—at the illness, at the doctor, at themselves? This is the longest-term challenge; to reconceive illness itself in more useful terms, to understand exactly what it is in relation to us, and to invent a medical relationship in which everyone involved believes and takes an active part. This isn't health-care reform; it's reform of health itself. If health-care reform still results in only 25 percent compliance, how much good is it?

Patient Progress Report No. 4

AUGUST 1992—The steroid inhaler ran out three or four days ago —it's hard to say. The inhaler still made a hiss when pressed, but the contents tasted different; I may have been inhaling nothing but propellant, which in itself may be an irritant. For the first few months I dutifully worked out how many days two hundred doses would last at eight doses a day, marked the date on my calendar, and got a new inhaler on that date; but first I discovered that the inhaler's effects began to run out before the two hundred doses had technically been used up, and then I began to experiment with six doses a day, then five or four, sometimes as few as two. Why do I vary the steroids like this, when my doctor has given me strict instructions to maintain a regular dosage? Because it saves money. Because I don't want to take more medicine than necessary. Because it's inconvenient. Because I forget. Because I think I know my needs better than he does. Because I sense that my needs vary with stimulus and that asthma is not a constant phenomenon. Because somewhere I have an unacknowledged hope that in time I can taper off entirely, forever.

I couldn't afford to get the prescription refilled: over the weekend I had $17 to last me until Tuesday, and the inhaled steroids cost almost twice that. So I stopped.

On Sunday night I wasn't sleeping well anyway. It's hot, the pollen count is high—I hate this season. By 4:30 I was aware of my breathing. It didn't occur to me that I was getting asthmatic; it was like realizing you're lying on something in your pocket, and not being able to ignore it.

Over perhaps forty-five minutes of turning from one side to the other the sensation grew. Which is odd in itself: what was I actually *feeling*? After all, the muscles are there all the time, flexing and contracting, I suppose. Why don't we feel our breathing all the time? Or would that be too much background noise?

Eventually I cupped my hand in front of my mouth so I could hear the echoes of my breathing, and heard the hoarseness—my first asthma in nearly six months. It was barely there, and for a long time I considered trying to relax and sit it out, but the specialist had said something about inflammation in the airways doing long-term damage if it goes unchecked. It's the dilemma: common sense says that any chemical repeatedly inhaled is likely to do some harm, or at least start doing less good; medical science says that it doesn't, and that the *absence* of the chemical will do the harm. Lennart Nilssen's photographs of deteriorating lungs decided it for me. Or maybe that's just another way of saying that I was an obedient patient and overruled instinct in favor of the advice of a doctor even though I don't fully trust him.

For once I'd left my albuterol inhaler in the car. I pulled on shorts and walked outside. It was not yet light, a beautiful morning, cool, dove-grey, soft; damp cut grass stuck to the soles of my feet. Instead of dashing over to the car, I slowed down, then stopped and looked around the farm. Not even any mosquitoes. The outlines and the muted colors of the buildings and the trees and the sky blended. A small patch of mist lay over the pond. A disease, like any inconvenience, is a form of education: without asthma, I wouldn't have seen this.

PART V

Investing in Illness

Sharks and Hucksters

S ix months after the attack, I ran into another factor in the care and treatment of asthma that I hadn't even considered: health insurance.

When the local public-radio station laid me off as their publications editor, I was automatically eligible to continue under their Blue Cross/Blue Shield group health insurance, as long as I took over paying the premiums. I could shelter under this umbrella for up to eighteen months, and by now seventeen of the months had gone by without my considering what to do next.

In this and some other respects, I still think like a limey: I keep forgetting that living in the United States requires constant acts of self-definition, without which one is in danger of vanishing. (Working in public radio, I was sharply reminded of this truth roughly four times a year.) It is literally unimaginable to me that in an apparently civilized nation one's basic right to reasonable health care can be taken away literally overnight, and it was only when my former employer notified me that I was shortly about to be shunted off the books that I realized that something had to be done.

Premiums for single-person health insurance, I soon discovered, were staggering—no wonder nearly 40 million Americans are uninsured—and the policies on offer were full of hidden tricks, catches, riddles, and exclusions. My basic right to reasonable health care had not only been taken away, it had been turned over to unscrupulous hucksters and sharks: it was as if my car had been repossessed, and I had to walk through every used car lot in the state to find it and buy it back. Finally, a friend mentioned that he had relatively inexpensive insurance through a national association of self-employed professionals based in Texas, and, grumbling to anyone who would listen, I gave them a call.

Five days later, a salesman called. Like most salespeople, he liked to talk while he sold, and he made the tactical error of telling me that the United States had the finest health care in the world. When I replied a little caustically that the United States is one of the worst nations in expenditure on public health among the nineteen industrialized nations and has an infant mortality rate that most Third World countries would be ashamed of (and I might have added that the United States leads the industrialized nations in the death rate of children under the age of five, in the number of children not fully immunized against major diseases, in the number of men with cancer, women with breast cancer, and all people with AIDS, and that a black man living in Harlem is less likely to reach sixty-five than a man living in Bangladesh), he applied the same argument that is often applied to U.S. public education: We only look bad because we're more inclusive than other countries, more heterogeneous. Our figures would be the best in the world, he boasted, if only the minorities didn't bring them down.

His claim is not only racist garbage, it shows a profound desire to redefine the word *public,* in "public health," so that it really means "second-class." (Some people use "public transport" and "public schools" with the same implication.) He clearly saw, or at least longed for, a society of "we" and "they" in which we don't have to take any responsibility for them. In fact, as events would show, health insurance is a means of making health care in the United States more *exclusive* than in any other industrialized nation, and in doing so it works around the clock to undo what democracy has achieved.

This theme of profitable exclusion ran throughout his presentation. One of the key ways in which his company was able to offer me such great rates, he explained *sotto voce,* as if bestowing the kind of information insider traders would kill for, was that they deny coverage to people who have congenital diseases of the heart, kidneys, and so on. My mind reeled. Always the writer, I mentally came up with a company slogan for their letterhead: We Care for the Healthy.

But the Texan company is not the only villain. The business of health insurance is business, not health. (The fact that the phrase "health insurance" makes it sound as if one's *health* is thereby *ensured* is merely a cruel trick of language.) After the salesman had left, my reluctantly signed check in his briefcase, it struck me that severing the means of paying for health into public and private, especially if the majority have private insurance, severs our entire understanding of how we see illness.

If an insurer were compelled to insure everyone, she would be concerned about risk in the same way as we are: she would want us to be careful with our health, to be informed, to be preventive, so as to reduce expenditures to a minimum. Instead, she is concerned about a risk in the sense of a bet: we are a good risk or a bad risk. Private health insurance is a kind of gambling, and by being able to deny potential applicants, the insurer is playing with a loaded deck with better odds, and by being able to set premiums the insurer is playing banker and setting the ante. If you haven't got the health cards, don't sit down at the green-and-gold table; go out back to the alley where the 40 million working poor are playing health-care roulette, where the ante is all the money we have, and one spin of the wheel can ruin us. And if our fortunes are ruined, of course our health goes down with them, and sooner or later we become a drag on the public purse or run up hospital bills we can't pay, which drives up hospital costs for everyone, and those who have private health insurance hate us because they see themselves paying twice, once for themselves and once for us.

About a month later, my new insurance arrived from Texas. Noticing that in the general preexisting-condition clause, the waiting period was a full two years (I'd never heard of one longer than nine months before; no wonder they could charge low premiums), I thought I'd call to see whether the asthma would be considered a preexisting condition. The agent had reassured me that it almost certainly wouldn't, but then again, I didn't trust him farther than I could spit.

The nice-sounding madam at the other end of the phone didn't know; she'd put me on to a "Top Gun," someone who'd know the answer to this knotty question. The Top Gun asked me to check if there was an "exclusionary endorsement" in the policy. Sure enough, the exclusionary endorsement had its own page, which I hadn't looked at carefully, perhaps because I had assumed that anything called an endorsement couldn't pose a threat I should pay attention to. "Will you read it to me, please?" she said in one of those KGB voices that involve neither a question nor anyone's pleasure.

"THERE IS NO COVERAGE OR BENEFITS PROVIDED FOR LOSSES DUE TO ASTHMA AND/OR DISEASES OF THE RESPIRATORY SYSTEM ON TIMOTHY J. BROOKES."

Even in my fury, I was struck by the slipperiness of their language. There was no endorsement here, only exclusion. And what coverage was excluded? Not "illness" or even "claims" but "losses": they are trying to prevent their losses, not my illness; an ill Timothy J. Brookes is not a human undergoing a temporary natural condition, but a loss, a ship going down at sea. The weird preposition on severs any narrative or logical connection between incident and claim, between me and them; there is no apostrophe to connect Timothy J. Brookes to the diseases, which have grown from mere asthma to anything that may afflict me, from my sinuses to my diaphragm: nasal polyps, emphysema, bronchitis, whooping cough, pleurisy, pneumonia, lung cancer. It's the language of distancing-oneself-from-responsibility, right from the first words, "There is no coverage" rather than "We will not cover," for the company distances itself even from its own refusal to be responsible.

My anger over the phone was met first by puzzled incomprehension—exclusion was, after all, business as usual—then reassurance. If I could ever demonstrate that I had gone five years without exhibiting any asthma symptoms or visiting a doctor for asthma, then the exclusionary endorsement, naturally, would be dropped, she said, proving once more that the company had nothing against insuring healthy people. When I pointed this out she segued into a well-practiced refusal to admit responsibility. "It's an underwriting decision," she said, but as soon as I asked her why the underwriters had made such a decision, she quickly made them vanish like a magician dematerializing a volunteer from a trunk. "There are underwriting guidelines," she said, waving the phrase like a colored silk scarf to show that the trunk was empty.

As to why the salesman hadn't mentioned this possibility, she verbally shrugged, and he slid off her shoulders. "I can't say," she said, skillfully summing up exactly what she did well in life. Nobody was responsible for anything, except me, who was responsible for making sure that my checking account had $121 in it during the first week of every month.

I called the agent, who finally admitted that well, he could see that this wasn't a particularly good policy for me, as if he had offered me a dozen and I had happened to pick the one that didn't fit.

It took four months to sort through other policies that attempted variations on the same cynical maneuver, find a plan that was more expensive but had no preexisting condition clause, and sign on. During those four months, I refilled my Vanceril five times at about $27 a go, seething with resentment not only at health insurers but at my family doctor, whom I could no longer afford to see, for having a potted palm in his waiting room. It took no effort at all to start seeing health as a luxury that was routinely being denied me and millions of others, to see my doctor as wealthy, rich, and smug, to worry about getting sick, to worry about how often I was worrying about my health, to contemplate lying and fraud. I instinctively doubted or at least questioned the doctor's judgment, the validity of the procedure, the expense, the time the results took. It was a classic American oversight fall from grace: I didn't feel as if I had been mugged; I felt as if I had been forced to become a mugger.

When I finally found a decent policy with no existing-condition clause, my entire attitude toward the doctor's visit changed. I found myself thinking, "I think I'll drop in on Dennis Plante and get this checked out," seeing him collegially, affably, chatting about this and that. It struck me that I had actually been very lucky. What if I had needed to go to the emergency room? What if my daughter Zoë had inherited my asthma and was also on this policy? I called a local pharmacy, which gave me a price list:

Drug	Capacity	Unit Cost	Daily Cost
Intal	112 doses	$40	$2.87
Intal N*	20 days	$52.89	$2.65
Proventil	200 doses	$27	
Proventil N*	20 days	$20.59	
Vanceril	200 doses	$33.19	$11.65
Peak flow meter		$30	
Stethoscope		$15–$25	
Nebulizer (rental)			$40 per month
Nebulizer (purchase)		$195	

* For use with nebulizer.

In other words, if she was a moderately severe asthmatic using nebulized Intal and Proventil, medication alone would cost about $1,500 a year. Add perhaps $250 for visits to the pediatrician and the allergist and $500 for three visits to the emergency room, and between us our asthma would cost nearly $3,000 a year, none of it refundable. No wonder that so many asthmatics in the United States are invisible, appearing only at emergency rooms to recover for a while, or to die.

SEPTEMBER 1992—As part of his general examination of my lungs, the allergist ordered me to have a chest X ray. I waited ten months until I could finally afford it. If I had had a tumor, it would have been the size of a Hubbard squash by then.

The nurse, who was having trouble maneuvering me into the right position in the frame, told me I had the biggest lungs she'd ever seen. I felt ridiculously proud; and walking back across the University Green toward my car on this cloudless summer day, I found myself grinning at nothing and nobody, thinking, "I see myself as having a greater-than-average capacity for happiness"—and at once was struck by the term *capacity,* and its sense of fullness, amplitude; and there seemed to me a connection between size of lung and size of—I was about to write "size of heart"—size of *expression,* between the capacity for air and the capacity for joy. I thought of the way we describe people with such an appetite for pleasure and imagined the actor Brian Blessed's huge laugh, surely full-lunged rather than full-bellied, his no-holds-barred bellow.

These are attractive qualities to me, but why do we never refer to them in terms of the lungs? The metaphor is strangely absent. We speak of full-blooded, full-bellied, big- and even great-hearted, of having the stomach for something or the guts, of a full-throated birdsong, and even use the phrase "of his kidney" to mean "of his stature" but never, as far as I'm aware, of being full-lunged.

And you'd think such a connection between emotion

and breathing would have made its way into the language because poor lung function has such a dramatic effect on our emotions and our appearance. The asthmatic can't run, skip, jump, dance; we're reduced to a hunched shuffle. We lose the confidence of calmness: so much asthma occurs at night when we're trying to relax, giving us tension and anxiety rather than peace and quiet. We can't be authoritative or fluent; we seem to retreat into ourselves, to be stubborn, hardheaded, willful, uncooperative. Our condition looks more like a behavior than an ailment. From the inside it makes it all the harder to adopt the put-on-a-happy-face remedy of the wellness instructors. We've lost our breath, and perhaps it's no coincidence that in Latin *spiritus* means not only "breath" but also "life" and "spirit."

As I write this, I cup my hand in front of my mouth and breathe in. I hear the echo of the hoarseness. Question: Would I even be writing this possibly compulsive self-examination if my breathing were full, clear, and easy—so easy, in fact, that it would never occur to me to use the lungs as a metaphor for anything to do with mood?

Investing in Illness

A sk any hundred men, women, and children on the street why severe asthma is on the increase, and ninety will say, "Pollution," nodding wisely or shaking their heads bitterly at the folly of the human race.

On the face of it, industrial and automobile pollution would seem to be a likely culprit. The main pollutants are thought to be ozone, nitric acid, nitrogen dioxide, sulfuric acid, and sulfur dioxide. How they actually affect the lungs is unclear, but it's thought that the sulfur and nitrogen dioxides emitted from wood- and coal-burning factories, which combine with water droplets to form sulfuric and nitric acids, known as acid rain, have a similar effect in the airways, combining with mucus to form corrosively acidic mucus. Moreover, in lab tests sulfur dioxide makes asthmatics wheeze, and both nitrogen dioxide and ozone can make even healthy people labor for breath. In Britain, these pollutants are taken so seriously that anyone with Ceefax, the television-text news service, can call up a daily report of the ozone, nitrogen dioxide, and sulfur dioxide levels anywhere in the country.

In extreme cases, there seems to be a clear connection

between filthy air and respiratory diseases such as asthma. In Singrauli, for example, the so-called "energy capital of India," the air is so dark with diesel fumes and coal dust that Daniel Zwerdling told NPR listeners that he could barely see a man walking just a hundred feet away. According to a local doctor, 25 percent of the population suffers from chronic respiratory disease.

There are two problems with the pollution hypothesis. One is that even though at least 70 U.S. cities every year routinely violate federal clean-air standards for ozone, with Los Angeles being the worst offender, in most First World nations the air is actually getting cleaner. When I was a boy, living in London, I remember being driven through one of the last of the sulfurous pea-soup London fogs, each streetlight appearing a few feet away and passing overhead like a yellowish stain. We may possibly be producing more sophisticated and insidious forms of pollution, but the devil we know, at least, is less potent than he was.

The other problem is that if pollution causes asthma, then you'd expect that the days of lowest air quality would also be the days when most people are admitted to emergency rooms with severe asthma. Unfortunately, that isn't true: numerous studies have tried to find a consistent, direct correlation and have usually failed.

In fact, the epidemiological studies of environmental asthma have turned up some thoroughly unexpected results. Between 1981 and 1987, twenty-six outbreaks of asthma occurred in Barcelona, causing 1,155 emergency-room admissions: the cause was found to be not industrial pollution or traffic exhaust but soybeans—or, more specifically, a glycopeptide in the soy dust that filled the air when the beans were being unloaded at the harbor. The Australian city of Melbourne tends to have asthma epidemics whenever thunderstorms strike in late spring, and other cities have discovered similar problems during storms. Nobody knows why.

This apparent impasse reveals that whether or not we learn something about an illness may well depend on how we already think of that illness. If we think of asthma as an allergic illness, we expect a fast response to a simple stimulus, thinking of the high-pollen-count days when suddenly everyone is sneezing and wheezing. Some asthmas are that simple, but many are slower, less apparent—an industrial disease relentlessly grinding down the airway linings until they are sensitive to all sorts of alien stimuli, not merely the peaks in local emission levels.

The more long-term a study is, the more likely it is to show that pollution is harmful in this gradual, complex, invisible way, especially to the youngest children. In studies over one to four years, asthma has been found to be more common among children living downwind from coal-fired power stations in both New Zealand and Israel, and near an integrated steel mill in Utah Valley, whose rate of hospital asthma admissions among preschoolers was double that of a neighboring valley that had half the particulate pollution, even though the latter had higher smoking rates and lower temperatures. (Twice as many children were hospitalized for asthma when the plant was operating as when it was not.) The more acidic the air, the greater its effect on the airways, especially if combined with exercise and/or cold. A three-year study in Helsinki concluded that concentrations of pollutants even lower than conventional guidelines may increase the incidence of asthma attacks, even though the pollutants themselves may well not trigger the attacks.

In the United States, industrial pollution overlaps with other factors, notably class and race. In March 1990, Dr. Russell Sherwin, a pathologist at the University of Southern California, studied the autopsies on one hundred youths, mainly black and Latino residents of South Central Los Angeles, who had died as a result of accidents and killings. Twenty-seven percent had "severe lesions on their lungs" and 80 percent had "notable lung abnormalities . . . above and beyond what we've seen with smoking or even respiratory viruses . . . much more severe, much more prevalent." He concluded that if the youths had lived, they would have had a very high probability of clinical lung disease by the age of forty. "These were pretty young people," Sherwin said, "and they were running out of lung." Los Angeles averages about 120 days a year when ozone levels exceed the federal standard; but not all Los Angelenos are affected equally. According to *L.A.'s Lethal Air: New Strategies for Policy, Organizing, and Action,* by Eric Mann and the Labor/Community Watchdog Organization, workers in the factories that produce the pollutants are exposed to the highest levels, and these tend to be immigrant Latinos, who are driven to find whatever work they can. Poor neighborhoods are far more likely to be chosen as sites for toxic dumps and trash-burning incinerators and are also more likely to have factories and homes side by side.

Meanwhile, it's thoroughly possible that *one pollutant, while not especially damaging in itself, acts in synergy with others, or leaves us more sensitive to allergens.* Japanese researchers have shown a connection between exposure to diesel exhaust and the prevalence of mountain cedar pollinosis.

Pollution from cars and factories almost certainly helps to create the conditions in which asthma and other respiratory ailments develop, but probably doesn't cause asthma deaths to rise at 6 percent per year—except, perhaps, in Los Angeles. It's not even the main cause of unhealthy air. For that we have to look a little nearer home.

When we think of air pollution, we almost invariably think of outdoor air pollution. In fact, the worst pollutants are the ones we grow up with and breathe as we sleep, the ones we shut ourselves in with, day after day—especially up here in Vermont, where for six months of the year we seal out fresh air, closing off all the doors but one, putting up the storm windows, tacking up the plastic sheeting, or shrink-wrapping the windows with plastic wrap and the hair drier. These are pollutants we call home: smoke from cigarettes, small soot particles leaking through the seams of the woodstove or billowing out every time we throw in a log, invisible emissions from gas cookers and paraffin stoves and heaters, formaldehyde from a new carpet. Even cats and dogs are, in a sense, polluters, spreading an invisible cloud of dander, hair, and skin cells wherever they go.

These intimate pollutants, unlike outdoor airborne agents, do turn up in the medical research, correlating in a statistically significant way with the incidence of asthma. Let's take cigarette smoke, for example. In June 1992, the EPA published a weighty report entitled *Respiratory Health Effect of Passive Smoking,* a cautious, solid compilation of research on Environmental Tobacco Smoke (ETS) published in the respectable journals.

The report found that, in levels equivalent to ten cigarettes or more a day, ETS makes children more likely to develop both allergies in general and asthma in particular. (Premature and low-birthweight babies are particularly at risk.)

The longer the exposure to ETS, the more severe the asthma. In one study of children of parents with a history of hay fever or asthma, at one year old the children of parents who smoked had no more wheezing than those of parents who did not. By the age of five, 62 percent of parents who smoked had children who wheezed, compared with only 37 percent of nonsmoking families.

ETS causes children who already have asthma to have more and worse attacks. This is probably not simply because the smoke irritates the lungs: as with outdoor air pollution, exposure to ETS seems to have a long-term rather than an immediate effect on the airways.

The effect of ETS is made worse by damp: in Vancouver, asthmatic children exposed to ETS use far more medication during the cold, wet season than during the dry, hot season—which is, in effect, a sort of good news: it suggests that the effects of ETS are reversible, the EPA concludes, and that decreasing exposure could prevent some asthma attacks; presumably it also suggests that moving to a drier climate might do us some good.

All in all, the EPA cautiously sums up, probably 8,000 to 26,000 new cases of childhood asthma each year are attributable to ETS exposure. The total number of asthmatic children whose health is significantly affected by

ETS is "hundreds of thousands"; the number who are affected to some degree may be as many as a million.

This is pretty damning stuff; yet the more I talked to pediatricians and family doctors and pulmonologists, the more I realized that this report would probably make no more than 1 percent of parents give up smoking, never mind replacing the woodstove with oil or electric heat or taking up the carpet. How much easier it is to define pollution as purely an outdoor phenomenon, and therefore not our fault—something to grumble about, but not something that we, as individuals, can change, not something that requires that we literally put our own house in order.

Pollution illustrates perfectly the fact that no man's health is an island. At one extreme, Chernobyl proved that pollution events can potentially affect the entire world; at the other extreme, a smoker can no longer claim that she can kill herself by smoking if she wants, that it's her life she's affecting and nobody else's. The twin facts that we blame pollution for so many of our problems, and that in doing so we use the word to mean outdoor industrial pollution, illustrate how strongly we resist taking responsibility for our own health.

Pollution, in our colloquial sense of emissions from cars and factories and power plants, is, certainly, a significant factor in respiratory health; but it is also too perfect a culprit, footloose and therefore hard to track to its source, insidious, invisible, or visibly filthy, lacking a morally convincing public voice. It is the communism of the 1990s, the all-purpose bugbear, the "Just Say No" issue of our time.

Those who don't blame pollution for the general rise

of serious asthma blame stress, and when I thought about it I realized that these two fashionable health risks are cousins. Both are human in origin, and thus both are ways of taking a first step toward accepting responsibility for ourselves and our world—but in doing so, we accept only about one four-billionth of the blame. Both allow us to avoid thought or analysis. Neither involves confronting a powerful person who might do us harm if accused; neither involves confronting ourselves. Of the two—pollution and stress—we're more likely to admit that stress is partly our own doing; I've never heard anyone admit to being a polluter. Both disperse guilt like an aerosol.

Many of the factors in the rise of asthma, or the stubborn survival of any disease, will be found exactly where nobody wants to look for them. We have usually invested heavily in the means of our ill health; it's not in our interest to look too carefully.

Or, if it is in our interest, it's probably not in someone else's. One person's misfortune is another's moneymaker. As soon as the timid lions at the EPA turned out *Respiratory Health Effect of Passive Smoking,* the tobacco lobbyists and prosmoking factions jammed the airways howling about "bad science" and the infringement of their rights. This book will barely have hit the shelves before I hear in no uncertain terms from the Vermont Woodstove Association, the American Consortium of Gas Appliance Dealers, Partners in Paraffin, and Friends of Formaldehyde. If I had cited evidence to prove that industrial pollution was the sole culprit for the rise in asthma deaths, on the other hand, nobody would have raised a peep.

Finally, if we think of pollution as the harmful impact

that humans have on the atmosphere, we have to consider including our impact on the pollen count.

Records have not been kept consistently for long enough to conclude that rising pollen counts may be a major cause of the rising rate of severe asthma, but a suspicious number of cities and towns in the United States have reported record levels of pollen in the last two or three years.

Hay fever and asthma symptoms start appearing around a level of 100 particles of pollen per cubic meter of air; typical spring pollen counts may range from 200 to 500. In 1991, Atlanta recorded a reading of 2,200. In 1992, Bridgeport Hospital in Connecticut reported 4,800. In 1993, St. Louis recorded a reading of 7,900 granules of oak pollen per cubic meter. Doctors in Long Island, New Haven, Fresno, and Boston are quoted in news reports from the same period saying that more patients are coming into hospitals and clinics, more people are suffering from allergies for the first time, the symptoms seem to be more severe, and the usual medications seem to be less effective.

Two caveats: not all asthma is triggered by pollen, and the pollen count—the number of pollen granules in a cubic meter of air—is an imprecise index: it can vary from one end of your yard to the other, let alone from one side of town to the other, and in any case it represents the sum of all pollens, of which most people are allergic to only a few. Attacks don't rise in severity as the count goes up, but the higher number does mean that an asthmatic or hay fever sufferer has a greater chance of coming in contact with his or her personal allergen.

All the same, this is not encouraging news, especially

if smog pollutants combine with natural allergens to promote more frequent and severe attacks.

Why is the pollen count apparently rising? On a given day, a high count is usually a function of the weather. Damp weather promotes mold and mildew spores; a cold spring may cause tree and grass pollens to be released simultaneously, instead of over a period of several weeks or months. A general increase, though, may be partly a man-made phenomenon.

We often think of the natural world as disappearing under a carpet of asphalt, but in many places in the United States suburban development brings the worst of two kinds of change: not only more smog-producing vehicles, but more pollen-producing lawns, shade trees, and golf courses. Fresno, California, for example, is cursed with poor air circulation, exhaust smog, and farm-belt airborne pollens, but recent years have added a spreading skirt of housing tracts with Bermuda grass lawns and mulberry trees. One doctor estimated that Fresno's pollen count rises 15 percent a year. Formerly arid regions in the Sun Belt are especially likely to be affected by Suburban Pollen Syndrome. Phoenix, Arizona, has similar problems; Tucson has banned mulberry trees and can levy fines of up to $300 against homeowners who let their Bermuda grass grow too high.

In short, any human intervention in the natural world can affect the atmosphere, which is both our most volatile and our most vital medium. The most sensitive of our tissues that come into contact with the air—our eyes, the delicate linings of our lungs and nasal passages—are constantly presenting us with environmental impact statements that we didn't think to require beforehand.

Canary in the Mine Shaft

I would have paid as little attention to occupational asthma as most other asthma authors if I hadn't been told about toluene diisocyanate just after I'd finished building some bookshelves.

Toluene diisocyanate, affectionately referred to as TDI, and its isocyanate cousins are a family of chemicals with a wide variety of industrial uses—toy making, boat building, refrigerator manufacturing, printing, laminating and insulating, foundry working, car spray-painting. TDI is also used in the manufacture of synthetic rubber, in paint mixing, and in urethane wood seals.

I'd run across them because I'd found that a single exposure to an isocyanate can act on the airways like a second- or third-degree burn acts on the skin: the cells are permanently disrupted. This leads to a chronic and long-term wasting condition similar to chronic bronchitis, or to a perpetual hyperresponsiveness like asthma, or both. In 1981, two police officers, neither with a family history of asthma, were ordered to redirect traffic around an overturned tanker that was carrying TDI. After thirty minutes, one felt his throat burning and eyes watering, and he had difficulty breathing; after four hours he checked himself in at the nearest hospital. The other stuck it out for eight hours; seven years later, both men still had severe asthma. Occupational asthmas provide the best evidence that asthma is not simply the result of inheriting faulty genes. By being in the wrong place at the wrong time, apparently anyone can develop reactive airway disease.

Wait a minute, I thought. I'd just finished urethaning a set of shelves I'd just made. I wonder if I've still got the can? I rummaged through my half-used cans of paint and found it: New Environmental Zip-Guard Satin Clear Wood Finish, with ENVIRONMENTALLY ACCEPTABLE in large red letters.

Zip-Guard is made by the Star Bronze Company of Alliance, Ohio. Yes, their polyurethane contains TDI, I was told, but it isn't dangerous: all the TDI molecules are chemically bound into the product and can't escape. Dr. Howard Frumkin, an occupational medicine specialist at Emory University, was less easily convinced. No chemical reaction takes place to completion, he said: some loose molecules are bound to survive—and as TDI can provoke asthma in concentrations as low as 0.001 parts per million, any amount of TDI is potentially hazardous.

But if my questions about Zip-Guard had reached an impasse, I'd unintentionally found a seething new field of questions about asthma. The list of agents causing occupational asthma is almost endless. In the natural world, vets suffer from exposure to animal urines and danders; food processors to shellfish, coffee bean dust, and various enzymes and proteins; textile workers to cotton dust; sawmill workers to at least half a dozen wood dusts; and laxative manufacturers to ispaghula. While 5 percent of the population at large has asthma, as many as 45 percent of workers in small bakeries respond to flour proteins, and it has been reported that almost every worker in the power plants along the Mississippi eventually develops asthmatic sensitivity to river flies.

It's not just a case of those with sensitive airways choosing the wrong profession: in many cases, the workplace is a dangerous pulmonary environment, period. One-sixth of the commercial buildings in the United States are "sick"—that is, at least 20 percent of the building's occupants suffer persistent symptoms that disappear when they go outside. Beyond mere unhealthy decrepitude, though, the workplace is where *new breathing environments are created.*

"The prevalence of workplace asthma is rising," said Dr. Joseph Jarvis, a specialist in occupational and environmental medicine formerly at the National Jewish Center for Immunology and Respiratory Medicine, "probably because the workforce is increasingly exposed to a number of irritants and allergens." Occupational asthma, which is barely mentioned in asthma books for the lay public, is now the most common respiratory disease linked to the working environment, the miner's lung disease of the 1990s.

The key to occupational asthma is aggressive diagnosis: the longer a worker remains exposed to an allergen, the worse the prognosis. If exposure continues for six months or more, there's a fifty-fifty chance she may be asthmatic for the rest of her life. Ideally, a sick worker seeks immediate medical help, an informed physician makes a prompt diagnosis of occupational asthma, and an understanding employer makes a swift commitment to help the worker to get away from the allergen, offering retraining and compensation if necessary.

The major difficulty with occupational asthma is that, sometimes with the best intentions, the government, the worker, the employer, and/or the doctor may collaborate to make matters worse. To start with, occupational-health-and-safety supervision was gutted during the Reagan-Bush years. In Minnesota, for example, there are more than one hundred thousand businesses and about thirty OSHA inspectors. According to the AFL-CIO, the average workplace will be inspected every eighty-four years.

Consequently, health monitoring is left to the person who is least qualified and least powerful: the worker. To substantiate a complaint, the worker must prove that he is sensitive to a specific allergen present in the workplace by taking a "challenge"—inhaling some of the allergen and demonstrating that it immediately causes measurable breathing problems. As most physicians are not equipped to set up challenges, and as it can be extremely dangerous to inhale allergens, this process is, in effect, a way of defending the employer while subjecting the employee to inconvenience and risk.

The employer is also in a bind. Many chemicals are such powerful sensitizers that they can provoke asthma even in amounts *too small to be detected*. Moreover, the worker may want to stay put, especially if the job supports a family, times are hard, work is scarce, or one's skills are not readily transferable. Asthma researchers from Italy reported the terrible case of a forty-three-year-old car painter who had developed a sensitivity to TDI.

"Although it was recommended that he change his job or stop using paints containing isocyanates, he continued his work . . . taking anti-asthmatic drugs both at work and at home," the article reported. "On Monday, October 6, 1986, at 11:30 A.M., he developed a severe attack of asthma while he was mixing the two components of a polyurethane paint. Taken to the hospital, he was dead on arrival." The authors examine the "grey glistening mucous plugs in the airways," and the "hyperplastic and disar-rayed" bronchial smooth muscle, but the true cause of death, his reasons for staying on the job, remain unques-tioned.

When I was typing up this chapter I dug out the urethane Materials Safety Data Sheet sent me by the Star Bronze Company of Alliance, Ohio, and took a closer look.

The sheet, which I'd tossed aside after reading that it didn't even mention TDI, made my hair stand on end: "Hazardous decomposition of byproducts . . ." "Can cause [eye] irritation and conjunctivitis . . ." "Ingestion: may cause gastrointestinal irritation and nausea . . ." "Chronic exposure may cause permanent brain and ner-vous system damage . . . concentrating and inhaling the contents may be harmful or prove fatal."

At once it struck me that these weren't only safety in-structions; these were *working conditions*. They came as a shock to me only because I've spent so little time in facto-ries, or paint shops, or body shops, or refineries. And I started to realize what the word *occupational* means—and, at the same moment, the phrase "blue collar" suddenly made sense.

Although some occupational asthmas (and here asthma is a stand-in for all occupational health hazards) strike in offices and even in boardrooms, the vast majority of them affect those who have not made it to that safe zone, and are still surrounded by the machinery and raw materials of industrial and agricultural processes. Disease is by definition intimate contact between ourselves and an alien environment, and while many occupational asthmas are provoked by abnormal exposure to natural allergens (red cedar dust, for example, or flour), industry constantly creates alien environments.

When I first came to this country, I thought the term "blue collar" was a convenient euphemism for "working class" in a nation that had used brute force to break the backs of the labor unions and now wanted to perpetuate the myth that it was a classless society. Thinking now about occupational health and safety, I find that "blue collar" seems more graphic, more apt, more a symbol of the extent to which power and health go hand in hand. The blue collar, after all, implies *protective* clothing, a working life in which dirt is only the symptom of a constant implied threat, of physical hazards that white-collar workers never face. (Police, incidentally, traditionally wear blue collars.)

And at once I find myself asking what if doctors wore blue collars instead of white coats? What if every medical student served a residency not in a hospital but in a factory? What if doctors saw firsthand not the symptoms but the causes of illness—the constant noise, the PVC fumes, the unguarded saw blade, the machinery that forced its operator to stoop all day, the lack of fresh air and sunlight—and suffered the same hazards? Wouldn't that start us turning out a different breed of physician, a different sense of the role of medicine?

Modern medicine has defined health as the ability to work—and, conversely, the importance of illness is often illustrated in terms of number of workdays lost, or the cost to a company. In such a climate, it is the doctor's job to get the patient back to work. This sounds fine—after all, who wants to be out of work?—but it ignores the fact that diseases typically arise out of context. The doctor who thinks she is doing the patient a favor by getting him back to work is not only returning the patient to the conditions that may have contributed to the ill health; she is also shifting attention away from the complex social and economic realities out of which the problem has arisen, and is redefining them in terms of individual pathophysiology and personality. A dangerous workplace is translated into a chronic bronchitis; medicine provides an alibi for social injustice.

A doctor is in a perfect position to diagnose problems in the world at large, but most doctors tend to treat only its symptoms.

Which is surely a shortsighted approach. The greater the separation between the doctor's experience and the patient's, the less the doctor will understand the full complexity of the patient's problems, and the more limited and superficial the care the doctor will provide. At this point it seems worth mentioning that only 12 percent of U.S. physicians come from blue-collar backgrounds; that the United States has a greater disparity between the salary of the average physician and the average worker than any other nation in the industrialized world; and that this discrepancy has been steadily increasing.

Occupational asthma is the perfect example of how dangerous it can be for the physician to think in patch-'em-up-and-send-'em-back terms. "Primary care physicians are not aggressive enough in treating asthma in general," Jarvis said, "but they *must* become more aggressive in diagnosing occupational asthma." Dr. Thomas Platts-Mills of the University of Virginia was even more forceful. "The doctor's first response should be to get the patient away from the site." Some physicians recommend this, he said, but "millions" of other doctors don't. "I think they should all be sued." It would be nice if a doctor could sign a prescription for education and retraining, too, but that's a battle for another decade, I suspect.

Whenever we decide that something is more important than health—and money and work are often seen as more important—then not only will our health suffer, but we will find ways of making disease invisible. As a species we have two ways of testing what we call progress: by its effect on our wealth and power, and by its effect on our immune systems. In the 1990s, our airways are the canary in the mine shaft: their inarticulate complaint is often the first sign that somewhere we have gone seriously wrong.

SEPTEMBER 1992—The day the ragweed season began, my nose itched and filled up. That night, sleeping badly, I found myself with a slight wheeze. I turned over, thought of something else—cricket, I think, and *Horton Hears a Who*—and after a few moments found that the wheeze had vanished like a small cloud of mist evaporating. But I was still tossing and turning, and after a while it was back, and I spent an hour or so nursing a patch of tension around my sternum. My neck, throat, shoulders, and lower body were relaxed enough: the tension glowed inside my breast like a flashlight under a pile of rags.

I got up and found that, like a fool, I was carrying around an inhaler with no albuterol capsules. I took a couple of hits of the inhaled steroids, which technically would do little or no good but couldn't hurt—such acts of self-medication border on superstition—and went back to bed. *Well, this is interesting,* I thought. *It's been quite a while since I had to wait out an asthma attack.* I sat up in the darkness, listening to the faint rasp like a father who has woken abruptly after midnight, thinking that he might have heard the baby coughing.

This is no good, I thought. *You're too self-conscious.* I remembered someone telling me about a guy who was asthmatic and gave his new girlfriend instructions that if he started wheezing, she was to start talking about something else—anything, as long as it took his mind off himself. I realized that this guy understood himself better than I do: he knew the asthmatic can become his own film and his own audience, making himself worse by his own self-awareness.

I let my mind play its Rorschach game, throwing up a series of shapes out of a dark pool, most of them formless and unrecognizable, falling back and re-forming until one suggested an avenue of recollection or fantasy, then another, and I sank back until I was half upright, my head propped against the wall, let my imagination run along each, further and further until I realized that forty-five minutes had passed and the asthma had gone.

PART VI

Beyond the Perimeter

However Improbable

Being a common but incurable disease, asthma has always been a challenge to doctors, who have responded with a range of treatments that are a tribute to the human imagination. Here are a few.

Ancient folk remedies   Ancient treatments for asthma show how easy the children of the 1990s have it, with their bubble-gum-flavored toothpastes and their cherry cough syrups. As an Egyptian asthmatic of the sixteenth century B.C., if you were lucky you were told to take a medicine of figs, sebesten, grapes, sycamore fruit, frankincense, cumin, fruit of juniper, wine, goose grease, and sweet beer, to be ground, mixed, strained, and taken for four days. If you were less lucky, you might be told to take the mixture that contained the dung of the idw-bird. If you were extremely unlucky (or perhaps extremely sick), you would be handed a papyrus prescribing boiled and strained colocynth, onion, hmwt, tjz, goose-fat, dsrt-beer, and decayed flesh. The dsrt-beer probably helped take away some of the taste of the decayed flesh.

The Chinese probably identified asthma even earlier

than the Egyptians, though I haven't been able to discover what treatment the famous physician Ch'i Po recommended in answer to the Yellow Emperor's questions. It was probably fairly unsavory. Some remedies used dried geckos. The poet Hillary Tom, who suffered from asthma during her childhood in China, was made to drink roach-gut tea. That is, tea made of the innards of cockroaches. "I cannot stand the smell of a crushed roach to this day," she told NPR's Neal Conan. "It makes me want to throw up."

I wonder if the Chinese knew that cockroaches were a potent allergen? If so, the remedy would be a perfect example of homeopathy at work. On the other hand, as an Englishman I must point out that this remedy stretches the definition of "tea" to an unconscionable extreme.

In classical Greece, it was thought that sulfur, which induces coughing, would help asthmatics cough up whatever was making them wheeze, so kindly guides led asthmatics up to the crater of Mount Etna to inhale the healing fumes. What is now called "medical outcomes research" was still in its infancy at the time, so it isn't clear whether more Greeks expired of the fumes or the climb.

American folk treatments have included licorice water, apple water, mullein, and a potion of gum ammoniac. Mind you, a century ago conventional medicine strongly favored the use of cocaine and marijuana. The poet John Engels recalls that his grandmother suffered from asthma, and he disliked visiting her house as a boy because of its strong smell, which he came to assume was just one of those old-lady's-house odors—until he walked into a college dorm in the 1960s and it all came flooding back, like Proust and the madeleine.

Acupuncture   I've always been interested in acupuncture, and I was seriously thinking of trying it, even though (or perhaps because) a hard-line allergist told a friend of mine, "Doing acupuncture for asthma is like standing on your head and baying at the moon." A review of the clinical literature, though, changed my mind. While acupuncture seems to help some asthmatics—hard to explain in Western terms—in a small number of cases it has resulted in pneumothorax, a condition in which air leaks into the chest cavity rather than into the lungs. As you breathe in, your lung cavity fills with air, the pressure of which can force a lung to collapse, thereby throwing still more strain on the other. You can suffocate yourself by trying to breathe. I don't even want to think about it.

Yoga   It makes sense to me that any discipline that involves relaxation and breath control would help at least some asthmatics at least somewhat, and yoga has a fairly good press among asthmatics. Can't possibly do any harm. I haven't given it a serious try because I'm at my happiest when I'm alert, vivid, my mind firing on all cylinders, and the few times I've tried yoga, I've been merely bored. Could that be part of the problem? Is this another sign that my sentry refuses to relax his viligance, even when ordered to take some R&R?

Altitude therapy   Mountain sanitoriums have long been used to treat respiratory illness—originally tuberculosis, of course, but also asthma. Several countries have high-altitude clinics; the most famous are those in the Alps, which were so fashionable that the town of Davos in

Switzerland had an English church and even a free English library.

A wide variety of studies have testified that altitude treatment is of considerable benefit to asthmatics. One especially convenient cohort to study was provided by the British Red Cross, which between 1954 and 1976 raised funds to send 212 children from the British Midlands to Davos for periods of between six months and two years. (The Midlands includes my erstwhile hometown of Worcester, and I would probably have been eligible, but as far as I know my parents never heard of the program— which was probably just as well: I'm not sure that any of us would have wanted me to go for that long. See parentectomy, below.)

Follow-up studies showed that most of the children benefited from their altitude treatment. While at Davos, about two-thirds were free from asthma in the clean, dry mountain air; on returning to the relatively damp and smoggy Midlands, about 80 percent remained better off, 122 returning to live a normal life. The unanswered question is why.

The common reason given nowadays is that dust mites rarely live above 1,500 meters, where airborne allergens, too, are scarce—but the children returned to mites and pollens in England, in many cases without suffering a recurrence of their earlier wheezing. To me, it seems more likely that living a sheltered, almost stress-free life under close medical supervision, breathing such healthy air, can break the cycle of chronic inflammation—of which allergy-mediated mast cell activity is only one cause. (See also speleotherapy, below.)

I wish I could spend a year in the Alps, but I can't afford it, and virtually no one else can either. More important, medical thinking in the United States is primarily pharmacological; altitude therapy seems immaterial, almost ethereal, to test-and-pill physicians, and therefore to health-insurance companies. Dr. Robert Klein, an asthma specialist who trained in Switzerland, told me that it is common in some European countries to send a variety of patients off to sanatoriums in the mountains—at the state's expense—where they have a complete change of lifestyle and diet, have minimal drug therapy, and enjoy fresh air, exercise, and physical therapy. The results seem to be good. "God forbid that we [in the United States] should ask someone to take three weeks off work," he chuckled. Or pay for us to change our unhealthy habits.

Balneotherapy Studies in Germany, Japan, Tunisia, Greece, Senegal, and Sweden attest to the therapeutic value of hot water, the German and Japanese studies suggesting that swimming in hot baths may be especially useful for helping older asthmatics clear mucus out of their lungs. (Swimming is least likely of all sports to provoke exercise-induced asthma, leading to speculation that breathing hard tends to dry out the airways, causing bronchospasm.) This comes as no surprise to me: I use hot baths for every ailment imaginable. Nothing seems so profoundly soothing, containing, and reassuring as the gentle, warm pressure of water on skin—it's really uterotherapy, I suppose—but it has never done much for my asthma. I can remember being caught without my pills once when I was a student and crouching in a shower in the middle of the night, cupping my hands in front of my face so they constantly filled with hot water, breathing the steam from my cupped hands, emptying and refilling them over and over. Didn't seem to help.

Hypnotism A number of studies suggest that hypnotism may help some of us with stress-related or psychogenic asthma, as long as we are also good hypnotic subjects. But there's no good evidence that hypnotism will help an allergy to peanuts, for example, enabling one's unconscious to set in motion a hitherto-unknown healing process that miraculously suppresses inflammatory mediators or pours oil on troubled airways.

All the same, it's an interesting possibility. Dr. John Heisse, an allergist and a registered medical hypnotist, has seen asthma as a result of embedded trauma, usually rape. He had a patient who became asthmatic only when she lay down under pine trees at her camp in the summer. He regressed her under hypnosis and discovered that she had been raped under pine trees. The asthma became a psychosomatic self-strangulation. "She didn't have true asthma," he said. "Hers was a cry for help." For such patients, he believes, both hypnotherapy and psychotherapy would be helpful, though hypnosis, if it is going to be effective, acts more quickly. "Hypnotherapy takes only a couple of weeks. By then you'll know whether it works or it doesn't work."

Breathing exercises Most asthmatics who see a decent doctor are taught to breathe from the diaphragm, which during an attack helps avoid the vicious cycle in which the labor of raising our chests to breathe causes back strain and makes even greater demands on the little oxygen we're getting. Breathing with the diaphragm also makes us focus on a point *below* the chest, which is a constructive distraction, and in itself is a common relaxation or meditation technique.

The actor-singer Paul Sorvino goes beyond this in his book *How to Become a Former Asthmatic,* claiming that asthma is "a mistaken breathing pattern . . . the body's way of dealing with allergies and stress." He recommends and describes a series of breathing exercises that have reportedly eradicated some people's symptoms completely and reduced others' dependence on oral steroids. He also recommends cutting out red wine (because of its tannin content), whole milk and all products containing whole milk, red wine, chocolate, and MSG to avoid buildup of mucus.

Sorvino's book makes some sense, though he never explains very clearly what a "mistaken breathing pattern" is, but I didn't do the exercises for more than a couple of days because, frankly, I lacked the discipline, and because the inhaled steroids were doing such a good job of convincing me that I needed nothing but them. All the same, I've felt for some time that I need some relaxation exercises, and I expect they'll include breath control. (See yoga.)

Speleotherapy   For decades, doctors in several Eastern European countries have been sending asthmatics to the salt mines—a treatment rich in symbolism and, by all accounts, remarkably effective. A colleague sent me a photocopy of a magazine article about a salt-mine respiratory clinic in Romania, its photographs showing grey figures singing, playing chess and even soccer in the converted galleries, appearing like ghosts from the charcoal depths of the mines, sitting grim-faced on grey benches—exactly the same as the news photographs shot aboveground in Romania, in fact.

Recent Chinese studies of cave-dwelling people in Shanxi found that the cave dwellers suffered less rheumatism, virtually no colds or infections of the ears, nose, or throat, and few skin problems—even their chickens laid more and larger eggs. Russian doctors have been experimenting with cave therapy since the late sixties and have claimed cure rates of 84 percent for chronic bronchitis and 96 percent for asthma, according to the London *Times*.

As with altitude therapy, it's not clear why this treatment should be so effective. Professor Peter Barnes, who holds the Asthma Research Council's first professional chair at Brompton Hospital in London, has suggested that clear air in itself would not make chronic inflammation subside in a mere two weeks: other studies in which asthmatics have been put in allergen-free environments suggest that the process takes more like two months. Perhaps the extra factor, he went on, was the fact that the treatment, in getting patients away from home and work, combined a stress-free vacation atmosphere with a strong suggestion that healing would take place. (The same would presumably hold true for a visit to the Alps.) This may not only reduce the role of anxiety in asthma but may even help the so-called "placebo effect" to kick in.

I was considering a visit to one of these subterranean clinics, but when I discovered that the most famous, at Wieliczka in Poland, had just flooded, my enthusiasm, too, was dampened. Western medicine might be expensive, nearsighted, overtechnological, and unholistic, but it rarely leaves the asthmatic five hundred feet underground with an aquifer rising around his ankles.

Chiropractic and other manipulative therapies I have a cautious respect for chiropractors, through whom I've finally learned how to keep my back healthy, after suffering intermittently from twenty years of chronic lower-back pain. On the other hand, the most egregious quack I ever met was a chiropractor in Maine who professed to have advanced so far in wisdom that he now practiced his art *without touching the patient.*

As far as asthma goes, the more evangelical chiropractors claim that spinal manipulation not only restores mobility to hitherto locked joints, but in doing so improves the activity of the nerves associated with those joints, so that in theory any complaint that might be affected by any nerve that runs to any joint in the spine—and this covers almost anything in the *The Merck Manual*—could benefit from chiropractic. My own chiropractor takes a more modest, commonsensical approach. Chronic asthma, he points out, often leads to a habitually hunched, tight posture that in itself restricts one's breathing. Chiropractic treatments can, over time, correct this posture and open up the chest and airways, he believes, which is certainly valuable, but they can't do anything for the asthma itself.

Experience tells me that a whole variety of activities can lead to tension in the chest, which can easily become habitual; manipulation can help break that vicious cycle, and retraining can, in theory, help us avoid it. Mental note: speaking of retraining, I should look into the Alexander Technique, a program of manipulation and posture training that may do nothing for the root cause of asthma but almost certainly does some good in terms of helping us to use our reduced breath more efficiently.

Parentectomy   Institutions, even those that work at valuable and altruistic endeavors, are often strangely silent about their early days: many a fine university or hospital was founded by a crook, religious zealot, or tobacco baron. The National Jewish Center for Immunology and Respiratory Medicine in Denver, one of the world's leading asthma research and treatment centers, at least admits in its official history that it owed much of its growth and prominence to "parentectomy," one of the most shameful treatments foisted on the sufferers of any disease.

According to the center's official history, Dr. C. Murray Peshkin, chief of allergy at Mount Sinai Hospital in New York, observed in 1939 that when a child with severe asthma was admitted to the hospital he or she frequently recovered very quickly—too quickly, in fact, for the medical treatment to have been responsible. This is an interesting phenomenon and one that is open to a variety of possible interpretations. At the time, though, medical opinion on asthma went as follows: (i) it is caused by allergies; any symptoms not caused by allergies are therefore caused by (ii) the patient, or (iii) the parents, usually the mother. (I'll come back to this subject when I'm feeling calmer.) In the case of the child recovering rapidly in hospital, it couldn't be allergies, because the child recovered before the allergic activity could be treated; it couldn't be the patient, because the patient, after all, got better; therefore, it must have been the parents. In some unspecified way they must have been abusing—or, worse, coddling—the asthmatic, and as soon as the kid was out of their clutches she literally breathed a sign of relief. Q.E.D. The cure: to get the kid as far away from her parents as possible, for as long as possible.

Peshkin's theory might have remained in the *idée fixe* stage but for the fact that the National Home for Jewish Children in Denver was casting around for a new role, and its staff noted that two severely asthmatic orphans had lost their symptoms remarkably soon after their arrival. The board of directors invited Peshkin to design a program "for rehabilitation of the child with intractable asthma, based on separation of the child from the parents' environment and the home environment, and his removal to the institutional program at the Denver Home." Peshkin went on to act as chief national consultant to National Jewish from 1940 until 1959. Presumably to give his theory scientific respectability (and perhaps as a grim medical joke with Freudian overtones, an ironic reversal of the cutting of the umbilicus) Peshkin coined the word *parentectomy* to describe the Denver program. This, then, was America's answer to Davos; it sounds more like Colditz, Germany's mountain P.O.W. fortress.

Let me be clear: many children's health improved during their enforced stay in Denver, and some children do indeed grow up in such dysfunctional homes that their asthma improves when they leave. I've interviewed a woman whose severe and chronic asthma was clearly her salvation in a home terrorized by her father: as the family invalid, she was never hit, was cared for by a concerned mother, and spent most of her time on her own, reading. She was, in a way, the family's safety valve: if she had a bad enough attack, as often happened during a mealtime, when the tension was at its worst, the fights might even be forgotten. But she was frequently rushed to the hospital, missed most of her schooling, and seldom ate: when she graduated from high school she weighed eighty-eight pounds. Subsequently she became the only child from her family to attend college (and, sure enough, her breathing improved once she left home); became a dancer, a teacher and a potter; and despite her asthma has fared rather better than her two siblings: her brother is an alcoholic like his father, her sister is a paranoid schizophrenic. To this day, she can't go into her parents' house because to do so would trigger her asthma; when she visits, she meets them on the porch.

But this is unusual, and there are a dozen more plausible reasons why a child should breathe better away from home, especially in a hospital or at a high altitude; nowadays domestic allergens would be the first guess. And in a way it is fitting that IgE, the antibody responsible for allergic reactions, was first identified by researchers at National Jewish—in 1966, two years after Peshkin left Denver after his colleagues insisted on research that would prove or disprove his theories, and the board rejected a fundamentally psychoanalytical view of asthma. Frighteningly, I've met dozens of people who still believe that a child's asthma is the mother's fault, and I can't help thinking that their education is National Jewish's responsibility, just as Duke University Medical School should lead the search for a cure for lung cancer.

Dowsing, or possibly exorcism Nearly two years after the attack I moved out of my apartment, which happened to be the back half of a duplex. By chance, my neighbor moved out at the same time. A month later, just before Hallowe'en, I got a call at my new house from a woman who had just moved into the front apartment. "You don't know me," she said. "I was just calling to ask whether while you were living in the back apartment you ever noticed anything . . . odd."

"Odd?" I asked.

She explained that she was a channeler and a psychic—and a graphic artist, she added, laughing, "so I've got my feet on the ground." As soon as she had moved into the front apartment, she said, she had felt uncomfortable, and on closer examination she had discovered half a dozen disturbing patches of negative energy around the place. Ghosts, in other words.

"Uh-huh," I said.

While these were not malevolent entities capable of wreaking havoc, she explained, they were nevertheless capable of affecting the health of living people who came in contact with them. She had invited a friend of hers, a dowser who specialized in clearing out bad energies, to help her encourage the spirits to leave this dull sublunary sphere and move on to the next stage of their journey— often, she explained, people who die suddenly feel their work on earth is unfinished and refuse to leave, or simply don't realize that they are dead—and, after two tries, the front apartment was now clean. Her friend specialized in this kind of work, she said: he had dowsed the home of a woman who apparently suffered from Chronic Fatigue Syndrome, and persuaded a number of spirits to move along; afterward the woman's vitality had returned, and now she was as active as ever.

(I should interject that while I'm not sure about channelers, I have a lot of respect for dowsers. There are a lot of them in northern New England—the headquarters of the American Society of Dowsers is in Danville, Vermont—and their inexplicable skill regularly finds not only underground water but oil and even missing people. They also refuse to charge for their services, believing their abilities are a gift to humankind. Cleaning up pockets of "bad" energy is a radical but not uncommon application of dowsing, especially among young or New Age practitioners.)

The reason she was calling, she said, was to find out if my old apartment was also haunted. Even though the front apartment was now untenanted by spirits of the departed, the stairway, which had no handrail, was dangerous for her two-year-old, and she was thinking of moving again. My old apartment was apparently available, but she wouldn't want to move in if it, too, was inspirited. She hinted that the people who had rented it after me perhaps fled so quickly because the place had made them feel uneasy. She hadn't been in the apartment herself, she said, but a psychic friend had, and she had sensed a presence named Daniel in one of the rooms, though he seemed fairly benign. "Did you notice anything odd when you lived there?" she asked again.

I thought of noises in the night and moments of sudden unease, and decided that my old apartment had been no better or worse than anywhere else. This question of health, though: could resentful spirits precipitate asthma—or could a severe asthma attack itself leave a psychic fingerprint, a disturbance in the ether? "Which room was this disturbance in?" I asked, giving nothing away.

"The little bedroom," she said, meaning Zoë's old room. I thanked her for her concern, she thanked me for my help, I wished her luck in her search for a new apartment, and we hung up. Feeling both relieved and disturbed, I went into the next room, where Zoë told me that Nickelodeon was going to call a thousand kids before Halloween, and if you answered "Nick or treat?" you won a prize. "But how do you know if it's Nickelodeon who's calling?" she asked. And she was right, of course: how do any of us know who will call, or what we should say?

Vitamin therapy   While admitting that evidence that vitamins help asthmatics is largely anecdotal, *Rodale's Encyclopedia of Natural Home Remedies* spends several pages quoting letters from people testifying to the beneficial effects of large doses of various vitamins, and "the full range of minerals." On the other hand, the book publishes testimonials to other remedies that the editor himself admits are perfectly ridiculous. This kind of scientific evenhandedness fosters a public confusion that perennially sells patent medicines and drives serious researchers bonkers.

Geomagnetism   A Czech researcher claims to have proven that the semiannual changes of geomagnetic disturbances in spring and autumn correlate with adverse influences in the cardiovascular system. From this pad he launches a hypothesis that a parallel mechanism of some sort is at work in the known semiannual variations displayed in peptic ulcers and, among other conditions, asthma. Although some pathological conditions have a complicated genesis, he concludes biblically, "In serious research it probably will not be possible to omit cosmic influences." Hard to know how to convert this into a therapy, though, short of spending half the year in space.

Avoiding dairy products I'm not talking here about the asthmatic who is allergic to cow's milk, but about the folk belief that cow's milk produces mucus. According to some of the more nutritionally assertive people I know, one cheese sandwich or a spoonful of yogurt can start one's lungs gushing like Old Faithful.

Why haven't I tried this avenue of treatment? For a start, I've found only one study that actually tested this evil theory (Haas et al., "Effects of Milk Ingestion on Pulmonary Function in Healthy and Asthmatic Subjects," *Journal of Asthma,* 1991), and it concluded in a rather lukewarm fashion that while nonasthmatics were unaffected by drinking whole milk, asthmatics did in fact seem to breathe less well in terms of one of the three measurements of lung function.

But the real reason is that I think I could happily live out my life on fresh homemade bread and Double Gloucester, with the occasional bowl of soup or bottle of good beer, even if such a diet is not ideal for the asthmatic. Reading the article in *Journal of Asthma* I felt my scientific objectivity crumble in an instant, and I pounced on its argument, crowing, *Nothing about cheese, you'll notice.* Not a bad word to say about Cheddar, the queen of cheese, nor about crumbly Caerphilly, chalky Cheshire, rich and assertive red Leicester, surprisingly little about herb and goat cheeses. . . .

Cross off the avoiding-dairy treatment. What's next on the list?

Eating fish   Ah, this is more like it. The April 1990 issue of *Prevention* (a publication to be taken with a pillar of salt) suggests that eating fish may help prevent asthma, diabetes, and other illnesses related to the immune system. An unnamed expert is said to have speculated that Eskimos may have a low incidence of asthma because they have large amounts of omega-3 fatty acids in their fish-rich diet. (I dare say that not many dust mites live above the Arctic Circle, either.) The article quotes Walter C. Pickett, a senior research biochemist at Lederle Laboratories in New York, as saying that it is conceivable (this sounds very much like a scientist, put on the spot, agreeing in the most hesitant and qualified manner to a proposition that he knows he can't prove to be absolutely false) that eating fair amounts of fish (starting early in life) may influence the later development of asthma. (Somewhat surprisingly, I've since found several articles in medical journals adding firm endorsements to this tepid assertion.)

This is more like it, I thought. I love fish. Reading this made me resolve immediately to eat more fish to make up for the fact that I'm not giving up cheese, and graciously condescend to drinking 2% milk. How about a diet of swordfish and brown bread and tuna and cheese and trout? And tomatoes. And the aforementioned bottle of good beer. This is the kind of self-deception that has made the human brain the marvel of the galaxy.

P.S.   Months later, after increasing my fish intake by about a kipper a month, I discovered that a high fish-oil diet inhibits cyclooxygenase (see aspirin) and is thus bad for those of us with aspirin-induced asthma. Is there no hope?

The history of medicine is speckled with individual, inexplicable cures that have enormous rhetorical power and suggest thrilling glimpses of uncharted medical panoramas. The plain, dull fact about asthma is that *almost anything sensible helps, but nothing helps enough to suggest a startling new understanding of the disease.* Improving one's overall physical and mental health is probably the best defense against almost any disease, even if we don't understand exactly why; yet most of us habitually mistreat ourselves in a hundred ways and give little or no systematic thought to our well-being. No matter how unorthodox a medical theory, then, if it has the effect of making us reconsider our work habits, or diet, or our ways of dealing with crises, or exercise, we will probably profit from it. I'm coming to believe that in its broadest sense, medicine is self-understanding.

In the end, the fact that we try some of these treatments—sometimes in the spirit of inquiry or of whimsy, sometimes desperately, with our wallets open and our brains in neutral—says more about us than about asthma or the individual treatment; and the fact that we don't try others shows how much stronger habit is than health, and how all of us have a little in common with the asthmatic who refuses to give up smoking.

Finally, one unconventional treatment that I did try:

Homeopathy   About nine months before the attack, I heard that a bassoonist with the local symphony orchestra had been completely cured of his asthma by a homeopath. I found his phone number and the name and number of the homeopath, and they stayed on a piece of paper on my fridge month after month, along with a recommendation to read Frederic Jameson's *Postmodernism: The Cultural Logic of Late Capitalism*. I actually came closer to reading Jameson than to contacting the homeopath. I had no strong reason either to believe or to disbelieve in homeopathy. The good news was that the homeopath was also an M.D.—a renegade—so my treatment would be covered by Blue Cross, and his background in conventional medicine gave a patina of safety to the enterprise. . . . It became something like going to childbirth classes: I knew I should do it, but the idea made me squirm. Besides which, as I've said before, we asthmatics prefer to believe that our illness will simply clear up by itself. I didn't go and I didn't go.

In the meantime, a friend told me that her daughter, at two, had developed severe asthma; she took her to a homeopath who treated her with sulfur and within weeks the asthma had vanished. Two asthmatic adults reported that their symptoms had improved somewhat under homeopathic treatment. At the same time I found myself reeling under the almost hysterical attacks on homeopathy from otherwise temperate members of the medical community who would clearly no more admit the possible virtues of homeopathy than the Harvard Philosophical Society would accept the existence of the Great Pumpkin.

As the months went by, Barbara despaired of me; in the end, I went to prove that I wasn't as self-destructive as she thought. The homeopath turned out to be a tall, gaunt-faced, taciturn man who, in my memory, at least, wore Birkenstocks. I, however, was invited to leave my shoes by the front door. He ushered me into his office and set me straight at once: he was not a traditional home-

opath, he explained, but a practitioner of anthroposophi-
cal medicine, which—in his explanation—was descended
from homeopathy but had been modernized and given a
philosophical framework by Rudolph Steiner. There was
traditional homeopathy, naturopathy, and anthroposophi-
cal medicine, and though he didn't speak ill of the other
two branches, I immediately thought of the arch-rival
gangs from the Judean People's Army, the People's Army
of Judea, and the Judean Popular Front in *Monty Python's
Life of Brian*. Still, I had heard of Steiner and was willing to
go along with all this—I'd probably make a great candi-
date for hypnotism—and gave him the most detailed
medical history I'd ever given anyone.

For those of you in the medical marketing field, this is
the way to win patients. He wanted to know if my asthma
was wet or dry, hot or cold, higher or lower, and whether
it came accompanied by cough or sneeze. He wanted to
know at what time of year it struck, and what time of day.
He wanted to know what I ate, what I drank, when and
how often I moved my bowels (this one always takes more
thought than one would suspect it should), whether I
smoked, drank, or did drugs, whether I was happy or irri-
table, intellectual or emotional. . . . He took notes for an
hour and asked me to return. I came back and talked for
another twenty minutes before he ran out of questions
and I ran out of minutiae. No doctor had ever taken such
an interest in the entirety of my well-being, and I had
never felt so cared for. Homeopathy or anthroposophy or
holism, this was all right by me.

It was just as well that his questions made me so
well disposed towards him, because his answers certainly
didn't. Periodically I asked him questions, and the answers

ranged from the not very reassuring to the bizarre. We see asthma, he said, as a kidney condition. A *what?* I asked. Could he tell me more? He thought again. I don't think I can, he said. You'd have to understand Steiner's theory of the astral body, and I don't think I can explain that.

He was on shaky ground, yet, in a strange way, his hesitation and imprecision made me like him. He didn't make extravagant claims or pretend to have all the answers; he made a refreshing change from the brisk arrogance of the conventional specialist. "I've had a fair amount of success with asthma," he said; and, later, when discussing what he would prescribe, "I've found that sulfur works pretty well." Homeopathy, it seemed, was based more on experience than on biological theory.

Homeopathy proposes that diseases should be treated by taking small doses of substances that produce symptoms similar to the diseases. The main purpose of homeopathic remedies, the anthroposophist explained, is to stimulate the body's own resources so that we heal ourselves; in that way, our immune system is encouraged to function at full capacity without relying on outside help, the problem is not compounded by the possibility that drugs might suppress the symptoms and thereby disguise a deeper problem, and we don't have to deal with any unwanted side effects caused by these pharmacologically potent intruders. Above all, by treating the patient holistically, homeopathy recognizes that one person's asthma may not be the same as another's; in each case it is part of an overall condition that has evolved in its own way and should be treated individually. I would later discover that homeopathic texts would discern more than a dozen different asthmas and recommend different remedies for each. In *The Family Guide to Homeopathy,* for example, Dr. Andrew Lockie writes: "Attack comes on between midnight and 2 A.M., person very anxious, restless, and chilly, thirsty for sips of water, feels better sitting up. *Arsenicum, 6cc* . . . Small amounts of phlegm coughed up, persistent nausea and perhaps vomiting, chest feels as if there is a heavy weight on it, *Ipecac, 6cc* . . . Asthma worse in damp conditions, often associated with early-morning diarrhea, *Natrum sulph. 6cc.* . . . "

I was nodding thoughtfully at all this like a neighborhood organizer for the Green Party, but in retrospect a little more objectivity might have been in order. On one hand, some "natural" substances are highly toxic—curare, for example—and on the other, the difference between "natural" remedies and refined pharmaceuticals is not as sharp as it might seem. Of the conventional asthma drugs, for example, theophylline is derived from tea or coffee, Intal was first extracted from a Middle Eastern plant, ephedrine is derived from the ephedra plant, and epinephrine is manufactured in our own bodies as adrenaline. The principal differences are that the doses recommended by homeopaths are (a) far smaller but (b) significantly less thoroughly researched, tested, and subjected to cross-examination by the FDA, which gives relatively little scrutiny to substances categorized as "nutrition supplements."

At the time, though, I was impressed by the logic of using my own healing powers in my defense, thereby improving my overall constitution and making me better able to stay healthy in the future; and the idea of addressing the condition rather than just the symptoms made sense. For once, I thought, I'm going to give the natural route a try.

The anthroposophist made me promise to cut down on dairy products (a tough one for me) and give up coffee, caffeinated or not, and then it was prescription time. He first wanted me to take a short course of sulfur pills—as a general restorer of the constitution, he said a little vaguely. And for the general sense of stress and mild anxiety I was feeling, some silver nitrate, which he described as "nature's Valium." ("Isn't that the stuff they drop on clouds to make it rain?" I asked, but he looked blank.) After that, I would come back and he'd give me some remedies specifically for the asthma. He warned me that many homeopathic remedies cause the symptoms to become more severe before they improve, then handed me my little bottles and wrote me a receipt for Blue Cross while I wrote him a check, pleasantly surprised at how cheap homeopathic remedies were.

Sure enough, after a few days I felt both more energetic and more relaxed, and generally much better disposed towards Rudolph Steiner than I usually am toward people who talk about astral bodies—which was just as well: when I went back to the anthroposophist after two weeks or so, he told me about the injections.

First, as I recall, was the tincture of *prunus,* or blackthorn, one shot into each side of the base of the neck. I can't remember why blackthorn or why that spot—because that was close to some gland or other, I expect. Second, the silver, one shot each side of the spine, between the shoulder blades, close to the lungs. I've no idea why the silver, and I'm not sure that he even told me. Third, the tobacco leaf, one shot over each kidney. He showed Barbara how to deliver the injection; she pretended to be cool about it while at the same time not watching too closely in case she passed out. The whole treatment was tougher on Barbara than it was on me, in fact: I'm not sure that I would have wanted to plunge a syringe into her back three times a week for eight weeks.

I'd like to say that I went straight off to the library and read several books about homeopathy, but the fact is, I didn't. Somehow my skepticism had been transformed into a dopily cheerful well-let's-give-it-a-try-and-see attitude. From then on, every other evening we broke the neck off the glass vial—a slightly dicey operation in itself, one false move and there were tiny fragments of broken glass on the bathroom floor—then I took off my shirt and sat on a stool while Barbara, behind me, looked for the right spot and built up her courage. She didn't mind the kidneys and the shoulder blades so much; it was driving the syringe into the base of my neck. When the prick finally came it was accompanied by little gasps, shrieks, and apologies; then it was all over, and we had to make sure that the glass and the syringe were thrown away someplace where Zoë wouldn't find them and start playing doctor.

We spent some nights at Barbara's house and some at mine, lugging the syringes and vials back and forth. Time passed, and my asthma seemed unimpressed by the remedy; the only change we noticed was that on the night when an injection was due we found ourselves more and more often at the house where the syringes weren't. Toward the end of the sixth week her stabs had become so tentative that the needle started bouncing off my skin. For the first time, I began to protest: I didn't mind one prick, but four or five, followed by a long, slow press that finally broke the skin. . . . Somehow it was remarkably easy for me to decide that these shots were clearly doing no good, and it was even easier for her to agree. We gave up, a little guiltily—who knew what might have happened if we'd just kept going for the last two weeks?—but nothing on earth was getting us to go through that again.

Our faith in alternative medicine echoes the creed of an earlier doctor, Sir Arthur Conan Doyle, that when you have eliminated the impossible, whatever remains, however improbable, is the truth. If Western medicine claims that a cure is impossible, we're straight off into the realms of the improbable, sniffing along the trail laid by none other than Sherlock Holmes. This is a logical fallacy, of course—just because orthodox Western medicine has no cure, it doesn't mean that no one else does, either—but if the local M.D. can't do it, then it takes no more than optimism to ferry us into the colorful land of the unlicensed and the unproven, and the hooting derision of the crowd in the white lab coats standing on the shore behind us makes us only more determined to prove them wrong.

A year after the attack, I finally got around to interviewing the bassoonist whose alleged miraculous and total recovery had aroused my interest in homeopathy in the first place. It was a disappointment. His asthma had not been especially severe to start with—his main complaint was exercise-induced asthma in cold weather and allergy to cats—and had not been especially well treated by conventional medicine. His treatment by the anthroposophist had not been swift and successful but lengthy and arduous. He had started taking Ephedra Plus for hay fever symptoms, then moved on to drops of Super Echinacea (a prairie plant, crushed, costly, which he described as "very vile to the taste buds") two or three times a day, for general tiredness and to boost his immune system. Next came the injections, first the course of *prunus,* tobacco leaf, and silver in base of neck, between shoulder blades, and over kidneys ("Every so often I'd stick a nerve," added his wife, who had administered the shots), then a course of what the label described as *"cuprum. ren."* ("It's an abbreviation for something," he explained), and finally, after being given thyme oil to rub on his chest ("It was messy and greasy and smelly . . . hideous stuff"), a course of injections of *stibium arsenicum.*

(Listening to his tale of perseverance, I was struck by his faith—or perhaps his gullibility—and, to a lesser extent, by my own. I know that nicotine is extremely toxic, that the nicotine of a single cigarette would be fatal several times over if injected straight into the bloodstream, and yet that hadn't even occurred to me when I agreed to the shots. On the other hand, this trust is a perfectly familiar part of medicine—after all, I don't know any more about the pharmacology of, say, tetracycline than I do of blackthorn. Trust is, in fact, an active medical principle; it is the basis of the placebo effect. What if the bassoonist's trust alone had caused the improvement in his asthma, and his ordeal of the series of eye-of-newt-wool-of-bat remedies had served mainly to cement his faith, following the familiar belief that if it tastes horrible, it must be good for you? Now we are entering the new and uncertain field of psychoneuroimmunology, where minds can cure or kill bodies, and everyone is groping in the dark.)

At some stage in the treatment, the bassoonist took allium for his allergy to cats, which didn't work ("You were as sick as I've ever seen you," his wife observed), and at several points he felt that he was getting worse rather than improving. Nevertheless, after perhaps eighteen months he noticed gradual, then distinct improvement. He is now virtually free of symptoms. It must be said, though, that he now exercises faithfully, takes time to warm up before running, continues to take some herbal remedies, and has made radical alterations to his diet, cutting out caffeinated tea, coffee, red meat, and most dairy products. The exercise and dietary changes would on their own produce improvement in some asthmatics.

A few days later, I called the anthroposophist's office and spoke to his partner. Why tobacco leaf? I asked. Homeopathy is based on the theory that like cures like, he said. Ye-es, I said, thinking that, with a certain stretch of the imagination, a lung might look like a tobacco leaf. Well, he went on, the tobacco leaf has larger pores than any other plant. It *breathes* more than any other plant. We think that there must be some connection between that and human breathing, the fact that it helps us to breathe better.

At that point I realized that I had had enough. I simply couldn't swallow the idea of submitting to a course of treatment that the patient doesn't understand and the physician can't explain. That isn't medicine, that's superstition.

But even as I write this, my heart sinks. *Nobody* understands medicine. Conventional medicine may subject its theories to tougher scrutiny and lash them to the rack of a more demanding syntax, but all too often the only evidence is *it has worked in the past*. When article after article in the medical journals repeats "crossover, double-blind, placebo-controlled trial," it is both a sign of scrupulous research and a kind of incantation evoking trust. Pursue any question far enough and you run up against "etiology uncertain" and "mechanism not well understood." Most of the major questions, from "What causes asthma?" to "Is there a soul?," remain unanswered; and yet, let's face it, it is not only alternative medicine that asks the patient to obey without question. An element of faith is required of all of us, physicians and patients, and we are never as angry as when that faith is abused.

Patient Progress Report No. 7

FEBRUARY 1993—Two signs that my general pulmonary health is better than it has been in a decade.

As soon as the weather started getting cold in earnest, I developed bronchitis: almost a tautology. Ever since I was sixteen this has been an annual event, a Twelfth Night, a tearing-down of the decorations, New Year's Eve spent coughing in an armchair. This year, amazingly, I dodged the bullet; or rather, it struck me at the base of the throat, and I felt the familiar burning; but then the bullet inexplicably melted. One day I could barely drag myself around the house and leaned back on my pillows to try to relax my chest, thinking, that's it: the infection will trigger constant asthma, I'll have to take oral prednisone again, as I did this time last year, and I'll be back in the drug war. But I put myself back on the full eight doses of inhaled steroids, and by the following morning my breathing had cleared up and the infection seemed to have eased. I could scarcely believe my luck.

Yesterday was a good test of how well inhaled steroids reduce the risk of cold-air asthma: it was eight below zero Fahrenheit with a windchill of thirty to forty below.

For the past ten years or more, the combination of cold air and exercise in heavy, restrictive clothing has made me steadily shorter of breath. (This, by the way, is one asthma that has typically passed quite quickly of its own accord once I've got indoors and taken my coat off.) In Vermont, shoveling out the car first thing in the morning after the city snowplow has left a three-foot bank of packed snow, ice, earth, and gravel is a perfect example of a localized asthma risk—not occupational asthma, exactly: more like indigenous asthma.

It was so cold this morning that in walking a quarter of a mile across town I hefted Zoë, a tall, robust six-year-old, up on my back so she was sheltered from the wind and could use both mittens to cover her cheeks, which, like mine, were burning with cold. For once, I had taken my albuterol with me, transferring it from my washing-tackle bag to my coat pocket, but in the end I cleared my throat only a few times, and by the time we made it back to the car I was quietly ecstatic.

I had to go out again that night, and in trudging home over the squeaking snow I remembered the advice that some expert had written on cold-air asthma: breathe in through the nose, so the air is warmer and less dry by the time it hits the bronchi, and provokes less reaction. Well, thanks, doc—we'll let you know. In fact, at temperatures lower than about ten below zero Fahrenheit the air is so cold that it instantly freezes your nostril hairs and after two or three inhalations starts sending shocks of pain through your sinuses into your brain. My recommendation is to wear a scarf over your nose and mouth, and/or to curl the tip of your tongue against the roof of your mouth so the incoming air deflects off the underneath of your tongue and the insides of your cheeks before diving towards the trembling airways of the lungs.

At times like this, the only consolation is that things are no better in Hawaii. Because the islands are so constantly and enviably hot, a pulmonary specialist told me, the entire year is a growing season, the perfumed air laden with pollen.

By the time I got home it had snowed some more, and I picked up the shovel to have a go at the end of the driveway before we got plowed in again. At least I wasn't wheezing.

Beyond the Perimeter

O ne reason virtually nobody gives for the rise of asthma in the United States is the rapidly growing gap between the rich and the poor.

The rise in the incidence of severe asthma in the United States, which can be charted from the late 1970s, parallels the steadily growing disparity between the increasing wealth of the wealthiest Americans and the increasing number of Americans who find themselves below the federal poverty standard.

Even more striking is the parallel between the rise in asthma among women and the feminization of poverty. Between 1979 and 1988, nearly a million families headed by women fell into poverty, until nearly half of the families headed by women were officially poor, a figure that rises to three-quarters among African Americans. Over the same period, asthma rates among women jumped dramatically. In 1980 slightly more males than females had asthma—32 as opposed to 30 per thousand, according to the Centers for Disease Control—but by 1990, 45 women per thousand had the disease, as opposed to 40 men. Most alarmingly, the number of women dying of asthma jumped 54 percent during the 1980s, compared to a 23 percent rise for men.

Asthma is one of the presenting symptoms of poverty. The fact that the wealthy also wheeze tends to cloud the fact that asthma is, in fact, a class issue. Studies in New Zealand, Scotland, and Britain have found that asthma is worst among low-income and one-parent families.

The asthma itself has a further economic impact, contributing to a downward spiral. A New Zealand study of ninety-three adults attending a hospital-based clinic serving "a socially disadvantaged urban population" found that "repeated hospital admissions and frequent asthma-related sick days contributed to employer discrimination, job dismissal, and lack of career advancement." Thirty-two percent of those currently employed said that they had difficulty getting time off work to attend the asthma clinic. Of those not working, 8.3 percent had lost their jobs because of asthma.

In the United States, of course, poverty is intimately associated with race, and the black-white gap, always wide, has been widening. In 1979, blacks were about twice as likely as whites to die of asthma; by 1987 they were three times as likely, with the death rate among black women rising twice as fast as that among whites. In 1987, asthma death rates in East Harlem were nearly ten times the national average.

Physicians have been aware of the possible connections between these figures, but doctors are not known for being politically radical, and most researchers spend as little time as possible studying the poor. The experts tend to be quoted as saying that "the mechanisms involved"—that is, why the poor should get asthma—"are not well understood."

In search of a better understanding, or at least an inkling, I called the New York Children's Health Project and asked if I could watch one of their mobile clinics at work among the homeless.

The New York Children's Health Project (NYCHP) was founded by the singer Paul Simon and Dr. Irwin Redlener, medical director of the USA for Africa Project and founder-president of the Children's Health Fund. In 1986, while Simon was recording his *Graceland* album, he and Redlener visited several shelters, including the notorious Martinique Hotel on Thirty-second Street, now closed. "We were astonished by the degree of squalor and the number of people living there," Redlener later said. "Sixty or seventy homeless kids were lined up [in front of] closed doors an hour before lunch, because the food ran out for those who came late." When Redlener asked a social worker what the children most needed, she replied, "Bring a big van with doctors in it."

Simon raised money, Redlener recruited medical staff, and the first mobile clinic was dispatched in 1987, since followed by mobile units in Newark, rural Mississippi, Dallas, West Virginia, South Florida, Washington, D.C., and Los Angeles. The New York Project visits each of twelve sites once a week. They would be happy to have me ride along, they said, and they felt it unlikely that my trip would be in vain: among the extremely poor, they said, asthma was virtually epidemic.

On a bright March morning, I drove into Manhattan down the West Side Highway, which like most of the approaches to the island seems permanently on the verge of collapse, a chronic state of mechanical ill health. I was once again amazed that in all the asthma advice and education books and pamphlets I'd read, and the TV programs and videotapes I'd watched, I couldn't think of one that had said, *Get the hell out of the city.* It's true that for some, moving is simply not a possibility, and that about half of those who move from one area to another to escape an identified allergen subsequently develop a new allergy indigenous to their new area. But the evidence is clear: asthma is worse in cities.

I had my first asthma attack in Worcester, a sprawling, brickish Midlands city of some seventy thousand souls, famous for its sauce, its porcelain, its gloves, its cathedral, the evidence of its Roman castle, its battle in the Civil War. Worcester was almost entirely defined by its past, in fact, but in 1964, shortly after we moved there, an entire section of the old city center, a maze of little streets running among a thicket of small, dirty houses, was demolished to make space for a series of shopping malls and a prestigious hotel. Dust hung over the city for two years or more as the ground was excavated. Countless trucks rumbled on and off the construction site while two cranes pondered over the chaos like mechanical insect philosophers. Worcester was surrounded by low hills, and my mother remembers standing on a hillside overlooking the city at sundown and watching the dust filling the air in the bowl.

In the same year that demolition began, I changed schools from a primary school on the leafy fringes of Worcester to a secondary school on the other side of the city. On most days my brother and I walked to school between brick walls and buildings that had long since turned black with deposits of soot, exhaust, and particles of tire rubber, through narrow streets where trucks rumbled and clattered, scattering marl and cement dust as they went, under the railway bridge as the morning train puffed overhead, its charismatic plume of smoke falling gently as soot on the pedestrians beneath. I had been making this two-mile journey for nine months when I had my first asthma attack.

My mother says that for the next eighteen months my asthma was so bad that she had to come and meet me at the foot of the London Road hill and help me up it. I don't remember that at all—though I remember the hill vividly, the blackened houses on each side, the trucks struggling uphill in a toxic cloud of leaded-gasoline exhaust and a chain of cars building up behind them in a slow burn of ozone and frustration.

Although you can't run from asthma, there are better and worse places to be asthmatic. A city debilitates us in ways that go beyond constant inflammation of the airways and a daily hammering of our immune system: it brutalizes us to the point where we start to assume that health is something that is only to be found elsewhere, and once we reach that point we may stop even thinking about looking after ourselves.

At the NYCHP headquarters on East Sixty-fourth Street I was introduced to the crew of Mobile Medical Unit 2: Ruth Headley, the registrar; Gustavo Velasquez, the driver; Winnie Font, the nurse; and Dr. Anne Lennon. We would be joined by Dr. Don Weiss when we got to the Skyway Motel, which, according to one of the large maps on the wall of the East Sixty-fourth Street office, is one of three shelters right on the perimeter of John F. Kennedy International Airport, home to some sixty single-mother families with 120 children.

New York is the only municipality in the country with a right-to-shelter policy under which nobody who asks for shelter can be refused. The homeless family system consists of some ninety shelters housing 5,600 families, including 10,000 children. A million people are on welfare in New York, and a basic fact of city life is that public assistance is not enough to enable one to rent a decent apartment.

The shelters vary enormously. Roughly seventy are Tier 2 shelters, offering apartment-style housing with private bathrooms, locking doors, and, in most cases, kitchen facilities—in short, a modicum of privacy, dignity, and independence. The other twenty or so (the numbers fluctuate as facilities are opened or closed down) are "welfare hotels," commercial hotels the city is forced to use for its overspill homeless population. In theory, these are being phased out, but the city is over a barrel: there are more families coming into the system than leaving. The number of families in the hotels has now risen back to about 1,150, including 1,700 children, and the Human Resources Administration (HRA) is forced to pay out over $2,000 a month to house an entire family in a single room of questionable quality.

In theory, the city cares for the welfare of homeless families in the shelters by providing medical and social services; in practice, both are a hollow joke. A nurse theoretically visits the Skyway part-time, two days a week. In theory, too, HRA provides a caseworker for each hotel, but seldom are these trained social workers, and grim tales abound of services being withheld capriciously, or sold in return for sex.

We headed out to the van, a boxy, thirty-foot pale-blue camper-style vehicle that takes up most of the block: a photograph on the wall in the van shows twenty-one employees of the NYCHP lined up in front of one of the Mobile Medical Units, with a couple of feet to spare at each end. After a quick stop at a deli in the high numbers to pick up sandwich lunches, the van crossed the bridge into Queens, crashing at speed from one pothole to another. Most of the medical supplies were in boxes on the floor, so they had no farther to fall.

En route to the Skyway, Dr. Anne Lennon told me she was doing her fellowship in child advocacy with NYCHP, at the moment the only such fellowship in the country; it is seen as a boom field of the near future, she said. She had trained in pediatrics, doing part of her residency at a hospital in the South Bronx. In many inner-city hospitals, she said, a patient may literally never get to see a doctor: some mothers simply can't leave their children long enough to wait eight or ten hours in line, and then wait in another line to pick up prescribed medications at the hospital pharmacy.

For a mother on public assistance, she said, the first responsibilities are food, clothes, and diapers: "Taking care of kids' asthma is very low on their priorities." It's not uncommon for NYCHP to come across young children who have had no prenatal or postnatal care, have had no immunizations—may have never seen a doctor at all, in fact. The food in the shelters is a constant source of contention: usually prepared off-site and reheated in a microwave, it's often completely unpalatable, Anne said. Many children refuse to eat it, and it's nutritionally doubtful. She is conducting a pilot study to assess the prevalence of iron deficiency, which among the homeless seems to be running at two or three times the national average.

We arrived at around ten, an hour late. Gustavo—Gus—parked the van on a narrow street running down beside the Skyway. The hotel sits between a crumbling superhighway, a long-term airport parking and storage lot protected by a chain-link fence topped with razor wire, the perimeter of John F. Kennedy International Airport, and a garbage dump.

"In the summer it reeks," Anne said. "We can't step out of the van."

Farther down the side street is a compound full of white dump trucks decorated with graffiti; above the trucks, the Pan Am building can be seen in the distance. We had been there less than five minutes when a TWA jet screamed directly overhead on its final approach: I couldn't have hit it with a stone, but it was low enough that I might try.

On the other side of the Skyway is the Airport City Diner, which looks as though it has seen better days. The Skyway also boasts a sign advertising the Pompeii Room Restaurant and Cocktail Lounge, but that has gone the way of the open fields. A tattered photocopied flier stapled to the utility pole next to the van's door reads "Free

Move into Storage"—advertising a business in Long Island City, but it might just as well be describing the progress of the residents of the Skyway.

The team converted the van, which was ingeniously designed. The driver's seat swiveled around to face a folding table and computer station: this became Ruthie's registration office. The passenger's seat turned and backed against the side of the van next to two other seats and opposite a third: this was the waiting room, complete with a VCR that played Daffy Duck, Porky Pig, and Woody Woodpecker cartoons for most of the day. Aft of the door, a narrow corridor bisected the van. On one side was cupboard-and-counter space, the nurse's station, with scales, a refrigerator for immunizations and the staff's packed lunches, a sink, and the usual support equipment—which included nebulizers, face masks, and oxygen so the staff could cope with a severe asthma attack. On the other side of the aisle were three rooms the size of closets—the shot room, a toilet, and one of the examining rooms. The rear of the bus was a second examining room.

Don Weiss turned up in an aging Volkswagen Rabbit. He stood about 5'8", hair slightly thinning, jean jacket, sneakers—he looked a little like a young, overworked Ben Gazzara. He trained in Newark and the Bronx, he said, pulling up his shirt and taking off an elastic back brace. In a hospital he worked at in the Bronx, he said, asthma is the most common reason for ER admissions, not only in pollen seasons. The city has enough allergens and irritants to make asthma a year-round resident; if anything, winter is the worst time, because of the rise in cold viruses.

When I asked Weiss how he accounted for the high rate of asthma in the Skyway, he blamed pollution, then the confined, congregated living quarters in which respiratory viruses pass easily from family to family. (Several mothers said that their children had gotten sick more often since moving into the motel.) It struck me as odd that neither he nor Anne saw poverty and the increasing strain on an imperfect medical and social system as causes for a large-scale rise in the rate of serious asthma.

Gus, meanwhile, was inside setting up appointments for the day. The NYCHP staff don't go into the shelters because, frankly, it's not always safe to do so. Though the shelters are nominally clean, some drug dealing goes on—one shelter is next door to a drug rehab center, and a lot of the residents are attending rehab but are still users—and where there are drugs there is violence. Last year the van was shot at.

The first patients came on board, and at once we began seeing both asthma and the constricting dynamics of poverty. Mrs. Green had lost her toddler son Harold's nebulizer when their apartment was destroyed in a fire two weeks ago. Medicaid refused to provide a new one. The boy, who had been using the machine every eight hours, had not had a treatment for a week and was wheezing appreciably. Mrs. Green had three children, all of whom had had asthma, as had both her nephews; the two older children, also boys, seemed to have "grown out of it." All three kids were nicely turned out in little warm-up suits and Nikes. To keep them quiet while four adults and three children were packed into Anne's "office," the floor space of which measured perhaps six feet by three, I squatted on the floor, sat one child on each knee and read

them *The Berenstain Bears Learn About Strangers*. It was a sur-
real experience, telling them that Brother and Sister Bear
"lived with their mama and papa in the big tree house
down a sunny dirt road deep in Bear Country" and warning them about talking to strangers. The kids on my knees
didn't follow this at all, and who could blame them? They
didn't have a papa, they probably had never seen a tree
house or a sunny dirt road, or a bear; and they were surrounded by strangers playing in the hall with them, new
ones every two weeks, trying to survive and make friends
despite their mother's warnings.

Estimates of the number of homeless children in the
United States vary from a quarter of a million to 700,000.
It's a rotating population, and one that fluctuates widely,
but it's probably conservative to say that on any given
night, 100,000 American children are homeless. Close to
20 percent of American children—nearly 14 million—
live below the poverty line, an increase of perhaps 3 million during the Reagan/Bush years. Children also suffer
under the country's barbaric health-insurance schemes.
Roughly 12 percent of all children under eighteen are
uninsured; for blacks the rate is 14.8 percent, for Latinos
26.2 percent.

One small boy came in for a checkup and more Alupent
bronchodilating liquid. His mother had had asthma since
she was nine; now both her children suffered. Her son's
was especially bad, she said, when it was colder or hotter
than average, when the household crew cleaned the
rooms, throwing up dust or applying carpet cleaner, or
when the exterminator visited. Her other child was in

school and suffered from exercise-induced asthma, which caused a different set of problems. The school refused to let parents leave medications on the premises, and budget cuts had left the school, like many in the city, without nurses, so when the boy had an attack, his mother had to walk to the school with his inhaler, the baby in tow.

A kid vomited on the carpeting; Gus was dispatched to scrub it up. Gus—stocky, with a dark beard and ponytail, wearing a clean white short-sleeved shirt—had already fixed the bus's water pump; driven us out to Queens; taken charge of traffic control and basic triage in the Skyway, escorting families out to the bus; and held kids on his lap while Winnie gave shots or Anne drew blood for her iron project. At some of the shelters he acts as a Spanish translator—all the NYCHP drivers are bilingual—and even a bouncer. The van is kept locked; from the addict's point of view it is, after all, full of drugs, and more than once suspicious-looking characters—single men, in other words—have tried to push their way on board. The Skyway doesn't seem like an especially dangerous place, I thought; but then most acts of violence probably take place in mundane locations.

I went back in to see Harold, who was still being examined. New-patient visits often last at least half an hour because of the need to take medical histories. Harold had been hospitalized once already. "When he'd be in the crib I'd wake up and not know he'd been having an attack," Mrs. Green said. "Now he sleeps with his mother." Anne carefully pronounced the word *Proventil,* but the mother knew it already. "All my cousins have Proventil." She admitted to smoking, though not, she claimed, indoors. "*I don't have asthma*," she said indignantly.

Like several of the mothers, Mrs. Green had smoked during pregnancy—an unwise move, as it hinders the growth of the developing fetus and may cause lung-specific effects as well, such as a reduction in lung elastin content. This, in turn, may diminish the newborn child's initial lung function, leaving him with a three to six times better chance of wheezing during the first four years of life. In the last two decades, *The New York Times Magazine* reports, the rate of smoking among women of childbearing age—between fifteen and thirty-five—has risen from 5 percent to 25 percent or more. In children whose mothers smoked before the child was three, the risk of developing asthma has more than doubled.

All the same, even as an antismoker I found it hard to condemn these women out of hand. If I ever find myself stuck in abject and helpless poverty for a decade or two—perhaps a generation or two would be more accurate—and manage to avoid developing any unhealthy habits or addictions, then I'll start criticizing.

A strikingly beautiful woman came aboard with her son Benjamin, a small, remarkably placid boy about four months old whose breathing sounded as if he was sucking the last half inch of the milkshake through a straw. A month ago he had had bronchiolitis, which should have cleared up after a week or so, but the wheeze still hadn't gone away as it should. "The lady across the hall said he had asthma and let me have her nebulizer. She said I could get one off the van. She needed hers for school." Benjamin's mother had been at the Skyway for eight months; he was a shelter baby.

Don Weiss listened to Benjamin's chest, which was bubbling on both inhalation and exhalation. If it were simple asthma, he should have wheezed only on breathing out. Don hooked up a nebulizer and filled it with salt water, which might help loosen the baby's sputum and give the doctor a clearer sense of what was happening. The mother held the steaming tube under Benjamin's nostrils; the boy looked around the tiny shot-room with wide but unalarmed eyes.

By now there were twenty-three people on board: three mothers, Ruthie, and seven kids sat in remarkable comfort in the reception-and-waiting-room area forward of the door in a space the size of the average family car. Ruthie and Gus gave out books and T-shirts with images of Don Mattingly, who donates $100 to NYCHP every time a New York Yankee hits a home run.

Carla Washington came on board, in an activist mood. A former basketball player from Bedford-Stuyvesant, she believed that if she could get a letter stating that her two children had asthma, she might be able to get her crisis worker to move her up to a Tier 2 shelter, where families can cook their own food and have their own bathrooms. She had been in the system now for six months. Although her family was from Brooklyn, she had been placed in shelters in Queens and the Bronx before the Skyway—such scattering is not unusual. When she was in the Bronx shelter her older daughter had a severe asthma attack, but Carla had nobody safe to leave her other daughter with.

(A shelter only looks like a community from the outside; inside, residents often have good reason to mistrust each other.) The ambulance was kept waiting for an hour before a family member could get over from Brooklyn to take care of the girl. "I'm very particular about who I leave my kids with," she said. "I won't leave them with anybody except a member of my family."

Thinking about her Sophie's Choice, torn between the well-being of her two children, I wondered whether with the notion that serious asthma is also likely to become more common as the divorce rate rises. If Zoë were asthmatic, the fact that her mother and I are divorced would unquestionably make everything harder. The added emotional stress and anxiety may or may not promote asthma but certainly provokes it once it has appeared. From the child's point of view, it would be only too easy to use asthma as a way of clinging to a parent at a time of upheaval in the suddenly half-empty house. From the parents' point of view, the logistics become a nightmare: Zoë would have to carry medication from one parent's home to the other; her mother and I would have to be in constant contact to exchange medical information, news of the most recent trip to the doctor—conversations that under the best of circumstances can easily be fraught with anxiety and blame, making the whole situation more difficult and therefore more dangerous. Divorce almost always leads to reduced income, which forces each parent to work longer hours and rely more on relatives, neighbors, and babysitters; but how can you trust anyone else when your child may need to be rushed to the ER at any hour of the day or night without warning? What could be more natural, if child care is not a possibility, than to feel compelled to cut back work hours or even go on welfare? And what if the parent has the asthma attack? I wondered several times what I would have done if Barbara had not been at my apartment. Would I have left Zoë sleeping alone? Never. I would have had to take her with me in the ambulance, I suppose—and that's a sight I would rather spare her.

Carla looked to be in her late teens; she still looked like the high-school basketball star, in fact. Children whose mothers are under twenty are almost twice as likely to have asthma than those of older mothers. It has been suggested that stress during the neonatal period may increase the risk for the development of allergy, but looking around at these young mothers and their lives, you could start making your own list of likely risk factors.

Little Benjamin was still wheezing, so Dan Weiss tried albuterol in the nebulizer. This made some improvement; mother and child departed with the van's nebulizer, another child diagnosed asthmatic. The NYCHP team carries a spare nebulizer, so that if someone needs one immediately they hand it out: going through Medicaid by the official channels would take two or three days, far too long.

Inhaled steroids are rarely prescribed for children under the age of five, Anne explained: the metered-dose inhalers require the child to be able to hold the inhaler properly and coordinate the squeezing motion that triggers the spray and, half a second later, the deep inhalation. In essence, then, these children, like their mothers, are in a holding pattern: the symptoms are being suppressed, but no long-term improvement is taking place.

* * *

While the van staff took a lunch break, Marian Campbell showed me the room she lived in with her three children, aged six, four, and one. It was small even by motel standards, perhaps ten feet by ten feet, the space taken up almost entirely by two double beds, a battered chest of drawers, and a television. The walls and ceiling were a number of dark, drab colors that defy definition. The air tasted *tight*—a dry, stale, motionless air, dusty and metallic. We went back out (it was hard to feel that we were ever in) down the hallway toward the cafeteria for lunch. Half a dozen kids were playing in the hallway while the cleaners went in and out of the rooms; through one door a crib was visible.

Marian had been at the Skyway for only a week, and was scornful of those who had been here longer; she assumed that they had entered the system not out of real need, but to cut the line for subsidized housing. And in some cases she might be right: at the moment 180,000 New Yorkers are on the waiting list for subsidized housing and will wait for up to twelve years to get in. A homeless family, in theory, will stay in the system for nine to twelve months and then be found an apartment. Marian would have none of this. She intended to be out of here and into a Tier 2 shelter within another week, she said—but then it emerged that she hadn't even seen her crisis worker yet; she hadn't been able to contact anyone within the system: she was effectively trapped in the Skyway with her children. "I don't travel by myself *period*," she said, then added, "I don't know *how* to get to Brooklyn." For someone without a car, in fact, the incredible truth is that *she can't get there from here*. There is no public transport out here, public transport in the United States being in about the same shape as public assistance, and for a second I imagined her gathering her family around her and walking off down the shoulder of the multilane highway—but this is absurd, of course, as pedestrians are bound to be prohibited.

At the cafeteria, bad news: the Skyway staff had said they would hold lunch for those visiting the van, but they hadn't. (Residents of the Skyway can't cook their own meals; they must show up at specified times to eat what the city has paid for.) There was only one turkey-bologna-on-white sandwich left, so each of the Campbell and Washington families would have to eat a pair of small, microwaved pancakes in Styrofoam boxes with sachets of syrup, a carton of milk, and an apple. Another box apparently consisted entirely of shredded lettuce. It was hard to see how this meal could cost more than $2 per head wholesale; it was much easier to understand the high rate of iron deficiency.

And perhaps more than that. Nutrition almost certainly plays a role in some asthmas, and if vitamin therapy may not be a cure, vitamin deficiency may be a contributory cause. One study, for example, found significantly lower plasma concentrations of ascorbic acid (vitamin C) in fifty-one asthmatic children. It didn't find a relationship between the level of ascorbic acid and the frequency or duration of attacks, though; instead, *vitamin C levels were directly related to socioeconomic class.* What this probably means is that low vitamin C levels may leave us susceptible to respiratory infections, which in turn can trigger asthma attacks or contribute to the development of asthma in a child. Even chronic asthmas often seem to respond to better nutrition, though it isn't clear why. To some degree, vitamin B_{12} seems capable of preventing the bronchospasm caused by sulfites in food. An Eastern European study suggests that vitamin C may help decrease airway hyperresponsiveness in exercise-induced asthma; a Russian study suggests that both vitamin P and vitamin C provide some help for some asthmatics, especially in winter. I checked to see how much Vitamin B_{12}, C and P there are in pancakes and syrup. Not much.

Carla picked up the theme of being trapped in the system. "The people who really need it, the system treats them like dogs," Carla said, gesturing at the food, the cafeteria, the freeway. There were no parks nearby to take kids to, she said, no day-care facilities to enable her to go out looking for work. She hadn't spoken to a crisis worker since last September and hadn't even been able to get hold of application forms for a Tier 2 shelter.

Back at the van, a deliveryman turned up to take prescriptions to a pharmacy and deliver them to the Skyway. Welfare families are sometimes turned down by pharmacies even if they have the proper credentials; sometimes the nebulizer arrives after they've been moved on elsewhere in the system. "God knows where the nearest pharmacy is," Don Weiss said.

The Skyway, though frequently referred to as one of the worst of the welfare hotels, is by no means as bad as things get. I didn't see any extensive mold or water damage in the rooms, nor massive cockroach or rat infestations; no knife fights or drug deals were taking place in the hallways—though this was, after all, the middle of the afternoon, and only mothers and preschool children were in the building. The NYCHP van visits once a week, which means these families are probably in some respects

better off than people living in the worst of the city's public and private housing. It's not as bad as some welfare
hotels used to be, either; one NYCHP patient, an out-
standingly intelligent boy with severe asthma, lived with
his family on the ninth floor of a welfare hotel without el-
evators. The stairs, needless to say, wrought havoc on his
breathing. When their room became infested with cockroaches, the management let off an insecticide bomb,
which triggered a violent attack. After that, the family
lived with the roaches, probably not realizing their aller-
genic potential; the boy's asthma remained so bad that he
attended a total of only two months of school all year.

At the end of the day, the worst case. A mother arrived
with twins, both born prematurely—after twenty-eight
weeks—and one with ghastly complications: hydro-
cephaly, congenital clubfoot, hernia, chronic ear infections, hypotonia, severe asthma. (Children of low
birthweight, multiple-birth children, and premature babies are more likely to be asthmatic, irrespective of race or
class.) The mother, who had a scar down her right cheek,
went over his medical history slowly but with considerable
knowledge of the details. At birth he had a "brain bleed,"
she said. What type? Don asked. "Type Two," she said. He
was now using a nebulizer with albuterol. How much?
"Fifteen cc of Proventil," she said. Don wrote out separate
referrals to eight different specialists. NYCHP would send
out a car to take the boy to each one: it's the only way to
ensure that non-van health care takes place.

    "I can't believe a kid like that would be at a shelter,"
Anne said.

"I can't believe he's alive," Ruth replied.

It was nearly five—time to go. Don Weiss, who had been muttering about exhaustion and burnout for the last hour, left without saying goodbye to the rest of the team.

The day, which had started out sunny, had become overcast and now rain started falling. As the van lurched and crashed through puddles and rush-hour traffic back towards Manhattan I thought, *It's just as well that we're not in charge of our own immune systems.* After all, several decades of constant thought and imagination have produced our current health-care system, our current social welfare system and New York's road system, and if our immune system worked as badly as any of these we'd be extinct.

Eight patients had presented with asthma, seven prescriptions for asthma had been written, but these were just the urgent cases; the basic fact was that *every single family that came out to the bus had at least one asthmatic*. The racial statistics, too, seemed to have been borne out: every child that had been seen was from a black family. Based on today's sample, which seemed to be representative, the incidence of asthma among children in the Skyway was over 50 percent.

Severe asthma is most likely to flourish when patients have no medical advice and supervision short of an emergency room. Controlling asthma, then, depends on the availability of primary care, but over the last twenty years, the number of primary-care physicians has shrunk to what even medical analysts regard as crisis proportions. The

Children's Health Fund has stepped in because the traditional supply of doctors has stepped out.

Even though the number of doctors in the United States has doubled in the last twenty-five years, large parts of the country still don't have enough primary-care physicians to provide basic care. (The definition of a primary-care physician is slightly elastic, but it's usually taken to include general and family practitioners, ob/gyn, pediatricians, and general internists.) In 1963 about half of all physicians in the United States were in primary care; now the figure may be less than a third, compared with more than half in Canada and Australia, and two-thirds in the U.K. American medical students, especially men, would rather go into one of the exciting new subspecialties like aerospace medicine or pediatric urology, or make a quarter of a million a year as an anesthesiologist in a suburban hospital—almost anything, in fact, rather than shoulder their $100,000 post-med-school debt load and stumble off into the inner city or out into rural America to be sneezed and coughed on for sixty hours a week, isolated from their colleagues, for maybe $40,000 a year.

Redlener himself has said that the mobile clinics are no more than a "stopgap measure." The question remains, Who is responsible for narrowing the gap?

A number of studies are being carried out around the country under the general auspices of the National Institute of Allergy and Infectious Diseases, to address the problem of asthma in the inner cities—developing culturally sensitive educational materials in English and Spanish, producing an interactive computer game for asthma management, counseling people on how to reduce allergens in the home and how to chart and manage their own disease, training a designated "asthma manager" to work in neighborhood clinics—but no matter how well intentioned or well designed these initiatives are, they're up against the basic and possibly immutable fact that the United States allows its citizens to fall further into poverty and ill health, and then provides less assistance to help them climb back out, than any other industrialized nation.

A final note: it may sound as if I'm one of those currently bemoaning "lack of access to health care," but the fact is, I don't like the phrase. I prefer words that prompt images, and the only image "lack of access" brings to mind is of a residential street in Basingstoke, England, that was severed by a new circumferential highway and became two dead-end half-roads. The problem with the lack of medical care for the poor is a little more complicated than that. "Lack of access to health care" is a sanitized, no-blame, let's-forget-history shorthand for "We Americans have never believed in universal health care, suspecting it of being a tendril of creeping communism." It's a problem that America at large has been creating steadily for decades. Is it any wonder that, like asthma, it is too complex for any easy solutions? Or that, like asthma, it may be rarely fatal but it is chronic, apparently incurable, and in the end can just wear you down?

Patient Progress Report No. 8

APRIL 1993—Last Thursday, I had to walk down to my ex-wife's house—my old home—to pick up Zoë and her skates. It was a tense quarter of an hour. By the time Zoë and I were back at my place my chest was thick—not wheezing, exactly, but with an accumulation of phlegm I spent the next two hours clearing. This remnant of asthma is a form of perception: it amplifies, in a sense, emotions that I might be disposed to ignore or suppress. It's a way of drawing attention inward—a way of hearing certain sounds that are beyond the audible range, a different kind of sound altogether.

By lunchtime I was exhausted: I felt as if I had been holding my breath all morning. What a primitive notion holding our breath is: it makes us mollusks. It's as if we could be safe inside our body-shell and danger would eventually give up and go away—as if our breath, which comes and goes out and in, is both what keeps us alive and what endangers us.

PART VII

New Dimensions, Different Landscapes, Strange Seas of Thought

Celestial Ankle

The wonderful advantage of not being a physician is that I can engage in research that would normally be professional suicide. With this freedom in mind, I went to see a psychic.

I'll call her Martha. I went to her on the recommendation of a friend who had recently lost her husband to cancer; she came back from Martha telling us about an astonishingly authentic reading, full of details that nobody but she and her husband could have known, and of encouraging messages from beyond the grave. I was curious. I'm the classic soft-center skeptic: I demand proof of everything but have an equally strong (if largely suppressed) yearning to believe that things are somehow more than they seem. What was more, ever since I was a teenager I'd wanted someone to tell me the kind of person I was and what my life was all about. I had more or less resigned myself to the fact that I had no choice but to find out on my own, but perhaps a little celestial guidance wouldn't hurt. The deciding argument, though, was financial. If this psychic knew about the spirit, why might she not know about asthma? And if she knew anything about asthma, why couldn't I define the visit as research for the book and write off much of the (surprisingly steep) consultation fee as a business expense?

When Martha called me into her office in a clean, bright, renovated New England farmhouse, she struck me as looking like a massage therapist: shortish, perhaps forty-five, greying dark hair, soft-spoken, but well-balanced and with an air of physical competence.

We tested the tape recorder, which seemed to be working. She settled into the rocker, folded her hands, closed her eyes, and said a prayer to keep evil forces out of the room, which rather unnerved me: it hadn't occurred to me that such things existed. Then she rolled her head from side to side as if to stretch her neck, but her head moved faster until the word *waggling* occurred to me; then all at once she stopped moving her head, started rocking back and forth, and began to speak.

At first she spoke about my work, my family. She sounded like a simultaneous translator: the language was curiously stiff, lacking colloquialisms—or when a colloquialism did turn up it was after a moment's search or a couple of less satisfying attempts. Sometimes her face was relatively expressionless, sometimes her expression would imply that she was struck by what she was seeing or saying, as if she was at least aware of this act of translation: she would react with a little pleasure when the right phrase came to her mind or to her lips, though her eyes remained closed for the full hour. Every few minutes her pillow would slip too far down her back, and she would hitch it back up; otherwise, she showed no physical awareness of her surroundings, though she, or whoever was speaking through her, was on the watch for anything I said, hearing my questions at once and answering them.

She repeatedly asked, "Do you see?" which reminded me of Donna Williams, an autistic adult I heard interviewed on NPR's *Fresh Air.* An autistic, Williams explained, suffers from what might be called a lack of intellectual proprioception: whereas most of us get a constant series of more and less subtle signals from the world to tell us where we are and how we're doing, how well we're understood and how people are reacting, she has none. She has to press on hopefully and check in the crudest manner: by asking. Perhaps Martha's constant checking was an example of a lack of cultural—interstellar, even—proprioception.

Virtually everything she said was perceptive. She gave the impression not so much that she knew a great deal about my family but that she was somehow meeting them for the first time as she spoke and seeing or learning things that she passed on to me, some of which were general observations that rang true, some of which were specific details that she could not have known by any normal means, and some of which were complete surprises that I had no means of judging. It was at times eerie, at times devastating, and at times extraordinarily reassuring, especially when she was speaking of (meeting?) my father and two of my grandparents, who are dead.

"Can you tell me about my health," I asked, trying not to give too much away, "especially my breathing?"

"We see that there is some damage to the lungs," she said. "There is a veil in the lungs, a greyness, a heaviness, a thickness—have you had this checked?" she asked, a note of concern in her voice. "We see this as an asthmatic condition."

Well, all right. She couldn't have told I'm asthmatic by listening to my breathing, but if she was working by guesswork she had a fairly limited range of possibilities to choose from. At my age, I'm unlikely to have emphysema.

"This is a condition that seems to have come from early childhood, but not that it was recognized at all times. . . . There are two things happening here, one of which is totally physical and the other of which is the emotional and psychological aspects"—fair enough, I thought, I'll buy that—"but primarily this is a physical condition that has been given to you and needs to be worked with."

She—or they—advised me to go to a drier and sunnier place; go abroad; spend time near the seashore; drink more pure (not tap) water and fruit juices; switch to either soy or rice milk. "We would suggest also the taking of a daily walk for even half an hour, if at all possible in the higher regions . . . to remove yourself from the city and go to a more country [place] on a daily basis, even if you have to drive there. . . ."

So far I was disappointed: this sounded like the advice of someone who had some fairly conventional, even clichéd notions of how to live healthily but knew little about asthma. Nothing about allergies, dust mites, chronic inflammatory conditions, Rolaids. I suspected that, whatever the value and the source of her information on other subjects, she was consciously or unconsciously infiltrating her own notions into the reading, and what I would get would be nothing but standard New Age dogma.

"We see that there is a respirator. . . ." (My inhaler, I

assumed.) "Are you doing this now? This must be done with caution, so you are not overdoing this at such a young age. We are saying that this should not be used instead of these other things, do you see? It is too easy, in other words, and you will need some of that later." My ears pricked up at the phrase "too easy": it exactly echoed my own thoughts on the subject—so much so that I began to wonder if she was not in fact a medium but a mind reader who unconsciously took my thoughts and translated them into a cosmological context that made sense. After a while I dismissed this theory; she said some things that I didn't know, and many others that actually contradicted what I believed to be true.

Meanwhile, I was beginning to see a fundamental flaw in this avenue of inquiry. Even if a psychic is miraculously able to speak to a congregation of benign spirits in some other reality who remarkably enough have our best interests at heart (or whatever organ approximates the heart, assuming they have substance at all as we know it), *what is to say they know any more about asthma than we do?* Oh, well: I had better just carry on with an open mind and see if what she said made any kind of sense or went roaming off into left field.

"But we do see this as a condition that can be very much relieved, especially if you will [give up] dairy products—although we see that cheeses are very popular with [you]. There are some that you would be able to take that are not of such heaviness. . . ."

This left me in two minds. The advice about dairy products is another cliché, despite the lack of much hard evidence to support it; on the other hand, how did she know I was a cheese fan, and of all the dairy products, I would have the hardest time giving up cheese? But by now she was already moving into less tangible matters.

"You are one who is carrying a great deal of pain. This is the psychological or emotional aspect [of the condition]. It appears to us that it is coming from early childhood, where you were not able to make yourself understood to friends, to family, when you were needed to be really understood." (My mother would later dispute this, arguing that I was a perfectly sunny child, but then again it's almost as hard to assess information from one's mother as information from a psychic.) "It is as if you stood alone somewhat and were one of great sensitiveness in the intellect as well as in the soul. Your friends were not always kind to you in this way. There was a great deal of grieving . . . it is held in the lungs as grief and pain. You do not like to cry . . . and you do not ever like to appear to be somewhat out of control in that which would be the grieving process. You have held back and held down—swallowed, so to speak— a lot of tears, and that swallowing has congested the throat as well as the lung area.

"We would ask you, as best you can, to allow this release to come. Do not feel that when you are in a hurtful place, or when you feel to cry, that it means that you will not stop, or that there is anything wrong with this. Crying is simply an emotion that is very similar to laughter, in some ways, and it will help to cleanse the lungs. You will need some practice in this, for you have been swallowing a great deal. Whenever you suffered injury to your heart's self or to your sensitive nature, especially in childhood, and in relationships, you swallowed the pain and turned it into anger, and . . . became easily frustrated and at wit's end and withdrew as an injured animal would withdraw and had [nowhere] to place this anger, and you did not allow it to go into the pain behind the anger, and consequently cry it out. It is just as if you have water in the lungs. You need to . . . allow [yourself] to begin to really feel that which is your pain and anger, and to allow [yourself] to cry."

Bronchial mucus as suppressed tears? It sounded like a Freudian theory, a metaphor being taken all too literally; but at the same time I found myself deeply shaken, on the verge of crying, as if she were right and I had been walking wounded all this time, hurt and baffled, not knowing how to relieve my distress, not knowing that relief was possible. What she had said—"you swallowed the pain and turned it into anger, and became easily frustrated and at wit's end"—reminded me so strongly of the collapse of my recent marriage that when she said "at wit's end" I felt as if I were standing in warm rain with my mouth open in a soundless wail while the rain ran down over my face and shoulders, soaking my clothes, draining down over and through my body.

"You are not one who is going to be able to simply walk over this asthmatic condition," she was saying. "There are those who are able to do that. You will be greatly bothered unless you are willing to deal with it—and we see that you are willing—in the physical ways we have suggested and also in the emotional and psychological aspects."

I pulled myself together. "Do you know what causes asthma?" I asked.

"Yes," she said without hesitation. "It is a weakening of the lung surface upon the birth of the child. It is almost as if there was not a sufficient amount of fluid or that which would be taken in in the early childhood—meaning not once you were born, but when you were actually in the body of the mother."

I was fascinated. What she said echoed the discoveries quoted by the EPA that under some circumstances (smoking during pregnancy, for example) the fetus's lungs can suffer damage in utero, developing with insufficient elasticity and leaving the newborn child vulnerable to all sorts of pulmonary problems. But things were becoming still wilder.

"There is also the condition of not having come through the birth canal quickly enough, [so] that the lungs then were congested, the lungs were not allowed to take in air quickly enough. It is as if there was a hindrance that took place in the coming forth from the—lack of a better term here—the belly of the mother into that which would be the outer world. Only momentary. In your case this is the case, and in many other people this is true as well. It is as if they did not come quickly enough, do you see? It doesn't mean here that your mother did anything wrong, or that you did anything wrong, we do not mean to say that. We simply mean that there are situations and conditions where there is momentary hesitation where the child is caught sufficiently long in the birth canal that they are not able to take the breath. It adds a congestion in the lungs and that does not open the lower portion of the lungs, as if it doesn't open but stays closed, stays . . . [she thought for the right word, then gestured with the palm of one hand over the other palm] *flat,* and creates a condition where it is never fully healed, it is never fully able to receive that which is the air intake.

"There can be other reasons [for asthma] as well; for

you it appears that you were not able to take in breath sufficiently quickly that the lungs were not fully opened,
fully expanded. There was some temporary damage that
brought on this condition as you aged."

The *birth canal?* By now I had gone well beyond left
field and was wandering aimlessly in the darkness of the
stadium parking lot. Then she gave me advice on how to
communicate with my father and gave me a message from
my unborn sons, and my last pretense of objectivity was
lost.

The problem with psychics is that we have absolutely
no means of processing the information they give us. I was
so overwhelmed by what Martha had told me that for
about a week I wandered around in a daze, wondering
about a newfound universe that overthrew all my old notions of time and space, life and death. Perhaps, in order
to maintain my sanity and some semblance of objectivity, I
had to distance myself from at least some of what she had
told me; perhaps it was simply that everything left me
wondering, *Could this be true?*, and her comments about
asthma were the only part that I could take to a reassur-
ingly credentialed expert and check. (Though this was not
as reassuring as it might have been: I ran the damage-in-
the-birth-canal theory past a couple of pulmonologists,
who grinned and shrugged and said, "Well, it's no more
impossible than some of the other theories going
around.")

In any event, over the next couple of weeks I put a
slight distance between myself and Martha's view of
asthma, as I had come to think of it. All that stuff about
needing to cry—couldn't that be said of most men? I even
ran a library check on the therapeutic value of tears and

discovered that virtually the only clinical research, by Dr. Susan Labott, tends to throw cold water on the have-a-good-cry thesis, recommending laughing rather than crying as a coping strategy, and dividing weeping into the Hydraulic Model, the Cognitive Model, the Moratorium Model, and the Proposed Integrative Four-Factor Model of Significant Therapeutic Weeping.

The whole event, I decided, had the golden glow of the undisprovable, that glorious Erich von Daniken quality of a hypothesis that hangs in the darkness of space or time, beyond history or measurement, teasing us with its lurid simplicity and with the slimmest of possibilities that it might be right. It's as if the SETI sky-watchers, telescope to one eye, sandwich in one hand, suddenly caught a glimpse of a celestial ankle—but whether the goddess was Truth or Deception, they'd never know.

The Nature of Suffering

Sixteen months after the attack, when my breathing was free and easy, I was down to three or four doses of inhaled steroids a day, my research was going well, and I was reasonably sure that I'd mapped out the territory that this book would cover, I strolled over to the medical library's computer, idly cross-referenced "asthma" and "emotion" and found *Asthma: Attitude and Milieu,* by a British psychiatrist called Aaron Lask, published in the sixties, back in the dark ages. This should be good for a laugh, I thought, and took it home.

The book is, among other things, a series of case studies that give fascinating glimpses of the ways in which asthma and emotions can sustain and express each other. Instead of arguing that all asthma is either psychosomatic or allergic, Lask seemed to be interested in the cases in which severe asthma refuses to respond to treatment. "The asthmatic invests a vast amount of primitive feeling in his illness; when the asthma becomes unbearable it is almost certainly an index of unconscious emotional conflict which forces him to seek help through the medium of the asthma. . . . Sometimes his personality becomes so firmly integrated within the asthma that the two cannot be separated." On an impulse, I looked at the publication date: 1966, the same year that doctors at National Jewish identified IgE and torpedoed the old canard that asthma was purely psychosomatic. Lask's book was probably the psychiatrists' swansong; after that it must have been tantamount to professional suicide to look for a psychological origin for asthma.

I thought my growing interest in Lask's comments was theoretical until he began to discuss cases in which asthma acted as a mask for a profound emotional conflict. The stronger the conflict, he suggested, the worse the symptoms. If the asthma was relieved, the symptoms of depressive illness often appeared: the asthma had both been caused by the conflict and acted as a distraction from it. By focusing on the (apparently) simple organic disease, the asthmatic could avoid the anguish of the unresolvable conflict in which he felt trapped. His suffering gave him a sort of alibi, and—to use a perfectly unsuitable metaphor—breathing room.

No sooner had I read this when two things happened: I felt a kind of sympathetic shrinking and constriction that can only be called mental asthma, and *I realized that in writing the account of my near-fatal attack I had left out something that had happened barely fifteen minutes before I started having symptoms, something so powerful that it had left me devastated, yet I had persuaded myself not to include it and then had completely forgotten about it.*

The attack had taken place during a grim time. A colleague in the English Department at the University of Vermont had suffered a heart attack and would spend the rest of the semester recuperating. Desperate for money, I had agreed to take over one of his courses, which meant not only that I was teaching four courses but also that I had to get up to speed on Restoration and eighteenth-century English literature, much of which I had never taught and hadn't read since college, nineteen years previously. I came to every class barely a step ahead of the students, convinced that sooner or later the shallowness of my knowledge would be exposed. On top of this, I was writing a radio commentary a week, a newspaper column every two weeks, and a magazine article a month; I had finished an article on deadline five hours before the attack.

As if this pressure weren't enough, Zoë's mother and I had separated fifteen months previously and were in the process of getting divorced. When we argued on the phone, I would get a sickening falling sensation that I think was the terror of losing my daughter, who ever since she was born has meant more to me than myself. When this happened, my first instinct was to take on the role of peacemaker, to look for compromise. Whenever I got off the phone, I felt lost and exhausted, I felt my spirits sagging, and almost every time I felt the tightness in the chest, the shortage of breath; but the crisis had been averted, it seemed, and I had done the right thing. When Barbara encouraged me to speak my mind more forcefully, I denied that I was angry. Zoë's mother was in some respects right, I said, and in any case if things got completely out of hand, who knew what would happen?

Moreover, ever since I had met Barbara, a year previously, I was acutely aware that as I became closer to her, Zoë might feel replaced and threatened, so my overall plan was for Barbara to enter my intimate life (and Zoë's) very, very gradually. If Barbara stayed over on nights when I had Zoë, she tiptoed out in the morning before Zoë woke up, or slept downstairs on the sofa bed. Needless to say, the situation was frustrating for Barbara, who felt like a third fiddle to both Zoë and Zoë's mother. I had made myself into the fourth fiddle, I suppose, but I didn't even think in those terms. Trying to look after everyone except myself, I felt as if I were being pulled apart.

That November night Barbara was working until midnight, answering calls on the SRS emergency child-abuse hotline, the last stretch of a fifteen-hour workday. I had invited her to stay over so she wouldn't have to drive fifteen miles back to her apartment, but as I went to bed, exhausted, my stomach acidic as usual, I realized that I dreaded her arrival. Would she want to talk about what had happened at work? Would she want to make love? And if I didn't, would she start up the old argument that I never had time or energy to devote to her and that she always came second after Zoë? With luck, I thought, I'd be asleep when she arrived, but of course I was far too tense to sleep. A few minutes after midnight I heard her key in the lock, and my heart sank. She came upstairs, and I tried to be welcoming, but I was as tight as a spring. "How was your evening?" I asked, wanting to cry, *Leave me alone!* She must have gotten the sense that I wasn't as welcoming as I was trying to be, and after a few minutes she went downstairs to sleep on the sofa bed. I felt relieved, I felt awful, I felt a ghastly hollowness. I was at my wits' end. My stomach felt as if something were trying to gnaw its way out. Ten minutes later, the asthma attack started.

* * *

Staring at Lask's book, I realized that I fitted his description of a "hidden emotional conflict" perfectly. What had he written? "When the asthma becomes unbearable it is almost certainly an index of unconscious emotional conflict which forces him to seek help through the medium of the asthma." Well, hadn't the asthma become unbearable? Hadn't it allowed me to put my own needs in front of everyone else's, confidently, urgently, and without guilt, for the first time in, well, years? Didn't it give me the chance to focus on something other than "the anguish of the unresolvable conflict in which I felt trapped"? In fact, by not only having the attack but then *choosing to write a book about asthma,* hadn't I given myself a glorious, enjoyable, and thoroughly worthwhile focus that enabled me to avoid thinking about my unresolved conflicts for sixteen months?

In fact, when I came to think of this book and asthma as a synergy, a pair of entities capable of influencing each other, it struck me how carefully—albeit unconsciously—I had steered my investigations away from anything that might infringe on my emotional conflicts. I had virtually ignored the role of the mind in asthma, and what I had planned to say was largely dismissive or safely factual.

My emotional agenda underlay my research and writing just as the hidden, imperceptible inflammation underlies the symptoms of asthma, persuading me that my feelings had nothing to do with my asthma. My difficulties with my ex-wife, my girlfriend, and my daughter were irrelevant; and besides, I should put their feelings first and respect their privacy. Anything I felt on the subject was beside the point; my job was to get the work done, earn the income, make life better for everyone. Whatever conflicts existed were nobody's business—not even mine.

I had never thought to try to describe the emotional landscape of an asthma attack; and it wasn't until the book was in revision, a week away from deadline, that I compared Lask's remarks with the psychic's comments on the psychological side of my asthma and saw how perfectly they fitted.

And yet—the cooler head prevails, the author takes a step back—in terms of knowing what causes asthma, or even what caused my asthma, this could all be coincidence. What my heterodox colleagues Lask and Martha say feels right—and, dammit, feeling right may not be a strong argument but it is beginning to look like a useful signpost—but I still have no proof of anything. Since the attack in November 1991, my asthma has improved beyond recognition; but whether that's because of the inhaled steroids, or because of some psychotherapy, or because the divorce has finally come through, or because I'm no longer quite as short of money or overworked, who can say? Too many variables.

When I looked to medical science to tell me whether stress could indeed cause asthma, especially an attack of this severity, the walls of the nation's hospitals and libraries began to resound with loud clunking noises. One doctor told me that, in his opinion, 90 percent of asthmas were allergic in origin; another said that, in his opinion, 90 percent of asthmas had some psychosocial component. Virtually everything anybody had to say on the subject was non-committal, evasive, conjectural, or plain wrong.

In fact, the first thing I had to do was throw out the term *stress*.

Stress is blamed for so many ailments that it seems as if it's only a question of time before we all drop dead from the sheer burden of living; yet it exists largely as a scapegoat rather than a well-defined medical entity. At times it seems to mean a kind of negative emotion, but none of the usual words for emotions—*fear, depression, anxiety*—quite fits. It can be used to mean a quality that exists in our surroundings independent of us (as in "a high-stress job") that can make our lives a misery, or to mean some psychophysical burden that we inflict on ourselves (as in "I stressed myself out"). Stress research has found it virtually impossible to connect stress to specific illnesses, and in fact our responses to stress vary enormously—in some cases we are stimulated, in others crushed—which is hardly surprising, given that the word means about fifteen different things.

The more thoughtful investigators have begun to realize this and nowadays say that the problem is not stress itself, but how we react to it. If we respond with humor, we're fine, and we may even benefit from the challenge; if we feel powerless, up go our levels of norepinephrine and our catecholamines, down go our serotonins and our T-cells, and we get sick. The problem is that this still presents a circular definition: if we respond to stress cheerfully, then in most people's minds we weren't stressed. In short, the word is so broad and floppy that even the sympathy of those who blame our asthma on stress is subtly unsatisfying, and we're forced to look elsewhere for answers.

The word *psychosomatic* is no better, though just as common. I was stunned at how many people still think that asthma is psychosomatic—that is, it involves no organic illness and is purely neurotic, like a nervous twitch. One of my students, hearing of my interest in asthma, said flatly, "It's all in your head, right? The medication's just a placebo, right?" An acupuncturist told me, equally casually, "Oh, it's all caused by your relationship with your mother." The very word *psychosomatic* makes me shudder, partly because of its callousness, partly because it is a reminder of the fact that this ill-informed and ungenerous belief was, until astonishingly recently, the standard medical opinion.

Asthma is somewhat unusual among illnesses in that with the arrival of the twentieth century our situation actually got worse. In the wake of Freud, researchers spent decades trying to establish a pathological "asthmatic personality"—a pursuit that continued well into the 1970s—or, failing that, an asthmatic's mother's personality. A steady stream of studies claimed to have found evidence that asthmatic children had been rejected by their mothers, or that their mothers were domineering and overbearing, or, on the other hand, doting and smothering. (Nobody seems to have considered that it takes a very balanced mother not to dote on a child with severe asthma.) Yet another line of attack claimed that some mothers of children with asthma seemed only to be able to accept their children when those children were ill, and thus subconsciously encouraged the disease. These were grim times for asthmatics and their mothers, and especially thanks to Peshkin promoting the concept of "parentectomy" and dispatching children to Denver, it's hardly surprising that the mythology of asthma still often blames the mother, whether for doting, or for smoking during pregnancy, or for having defective genes.

As a result of this blame-the-victim policy, the poor asthmatic became the automatic target for scorn and abuse. The best illustration of this contemptuous view of the asthmatic turns up in the character of Piggy in William Golding's 1954 novel *Lord of the Flies*. The antithesis of the officer-to-be Ralph, he's "very fat," shrill, bespectacled, asthmatic. He has lost his parents and in their place his auntie overprotects him, giving him a catechism of everyday perils to avoid: "My auntie told me not to run . . . on account of my asthma." His auntie (not "aunt," which might imply a brisk straightforwardness) has also told him to keep his windbreaker zipped up, and she has forbidden him to swim, so he has a fear of nakedness, of his own body, of his own masculinity: later we're told that he is the only boy on the island whose hair would not grow. Piggy is the stereotypical asthmatic child: intelligent but oversensitive, apron-strung, a mama's boy. In Piggy's case, asthma is a result of his lack of manliness, a continuing cause of it, and a punishment for it. He has lost the instincts and the abilities that will enable him to survive—on the island and, we suppose, in the jungle that is real life.

(The odd thing about the character of Piggy is that his character actually makes a fascinating argument for asthma as a vehicle for expressing psychological conflict. His asthma can be read as a means of concealing a profound trauma: the loss of his parents. Forced to suppress his anguish, desperate for sympathy and attention from adults, he develops asthma, which not only may make people feel sorry for him but will enable him to get out of the things he doesn't want to do—swim, run, be naked—because he has lacked a father who will teach him to enjoy them. The asthma is psychologically vital to him: if he were "cured" of it, he would be forced to face his grief, his insecurity, and his self-dislike.)

The discovery of IgE provided a clear, nonneurological mechanism for asthma, and at once psychological theory must have seemed like reading shapes in clouds. The massive pendulum of received medical wisdom swung so far toward objective—that is, demonstrable—causes that much of the asthma literature for the public now earnestly begins, "Asthma is not psychosomatic . . ." and many physicians deny that asthma has an emotional ingredient—sometimes by the logic that, as they don't know how emotions can provoke asthma, then they can't. When I suggested to the specialist that my attack might have been caused partly by stress he looked away impatiently, waiting for me to finish so he could get back to talking about allergy and inflammation. Nowadays psychiatrists get almost no referrals for asthma at all, except to counsel families that include a severely asthmatic child, whose illness at once becomes both an ingredient and a symptom of the complex dynamics of the family.

In the last decade the term *psychosomatic illness* has undergone a curious rebirth as New Age medical writers, who argue that our minds play a far larger role in our health than Western medicine has generally thought, have taken the word out of its closet in medical history, shaken the dust off it, and presented it in new, glowing colors. "Cancer and indeed nearly all diseases are psychosomatic," writes Bernie Siegel, author of *Love, Medicine and Miracles,* who claims that unhealthy states of mind are likely to promote illnesses such as cancer, and, conversely, various robust and vigorous mental states stand a statistically improbable chance of producing remissions and cures, sometimes even without medication, apparently by galvanizing the mysterious "placebo effect."

These intriguing studies, even if they are medically valid, have two shortcomings. The first is that they echo, in a kinder, gentler way, the psychological fascism of the Golding approach. If only you would smile, hectors Blair Justice in *Who Gets Sick*. Simply putting on a happy face may be beneficial, may increase blood flow to the brain and stimulate release of favorable neurotransmitters, he says. Be enthusiastic rather than cynical or hostile. Think positively.

You fucking smile, comes the answer. *You're the one who's happy.* If cheerfulness came so easily, Norman Vincent Peale would have converted everyone decades ago, and nobody would be ill or downhearted. As it is, despite his professionally cautious language, Justice sounds like an aerobics instructor yelling at us to pick up that serotonin level, kick out those stress hormones, stretch that immune system.

The second problem is that the connection between the mind and asthma is obviously far more swift and sensitive than the connection between, say, the mind and cancer—after all, I've had asthma come on during a five-minute phone call—but plays a part only in some asthmas, only in some patients. Asthma studies have nothing like the dramatic reversals of terminal cancer that seem to have been brought about by positive visualization, prayer, unquestioning belief in "miracle" drugs, and other mental approaches. Biofeedback and hypnosis and yoga and meditation and stress management show signs of helping some asthma patients somewhat, but not to the extent of spontaneous remissions or long-term cures. While illnesses such as cancer, heart disease, and rheumatoid arthritis may indeed turn out to be less exclusively "organic" than doctors once thought, asthma seems to have been through its "psychosomatic" phase and is heading in the organic direction.

And yet. And yet. The fact remains that under the vast smoke screen of psychosomatic asthma, there must have been a small fire or two. Anyone who sees enough asthmatics admits that some people do apparently start wheezing under some emotionally adverse circumstances. The difficulty is that we know it happens, but we don't know how.

The fashionable words nowadays for such asthmas are *psychogenic*—that is, originating in the mind—and *psychosocial*. They are a provocative mystery because they demonstrate not only how little we know about asthma but how little we know about the mind and emotions, and what part they play in our overall functioning. Many old-school doctors still tell their patients that anxiety causes hyperventilation, which in turn triggers asthma. This may be true for a small minority of asthmatics who develop asthma after shouting, breathing deeply, or even laughing, but as a general explanation it won't wash. Some researchers suspect that neurotransmitter imbalances could affect both mental and physical states; others suggest that the vagus nerve, which has endings in the airway muscle, could be stimulated to make muscles contract or cause mast cells to degranulate. (For my money, mast cells are unlikely agents in psychogenic asthma. It's too dry. The mast cell/allergy response, with its overflowing mucus-producing goblet cells, is much more juicy, sometimes overwhelmingly so.)

My guess, several researchers said, was as good as theirs—an invitation that seems to me worth accepting. Even if my conclusions are as unprovable as theirs, it makes a refreshing change in medical circles to hear what the patient thinks; and the fact that the patient thinks about his illness at all is a good thing in itself.

To start with the lukewarm: I don't think most of my asthma attacks have been precipitated by emotional upheaval, and I don't think there's such a thing as an "asthmatic personality." There are plenty of people who suppress their tears, and most do not have asthma. I suspect that many asthmas in many asthmatics are quite well explained by allergy and inflammation, even though those conditions in themselves still need explanation.

But.

My own history suggests as many as three or four different ways in which asthma has been at least partly the outcome of heightened emotion. To be honest, I still don't know what to make of the failure-to-cry hypothesis. It would make things wonderfully simple if it were true, but a metaphor is being severely stretched here: tears simply do not become mucus.

In a well-documented experiment, two groups of children, one of asthmatics, one of nonasthmatics, were shown a film of children suffering asthma attacks. The nonasthmatics showed no uniform, general reaction;

many (but not all) of the asthmatics began to have breathing difficulties.

This experiment shows the strange interknotted cause and effect in asthma: for many asthmatics—*but not all*—one of our most terrifying experiences is that of a severe asthma attack. If fear can provoke asthma, then fear of asthma can provoke asthma. By extension, anything that mimics asthmatic symptoms can potentially have the same effect, though such facsimiles vary widely from person to person. For years I started wheezing as soon as I swam underwater, as if the sensation of pressure on my chest were a threat in itself, or a threat of a threat. (I can't stand clothes that are tight around my neck, either.) A friend is sensitive to rooms with low ceilings, as if physical claustrophobia were a reminder of the internal claustrophobia of asthma. Maybe this is why some of us even seem to be sensitive to changes in air pressure. The foundation for psychogenic asthma of this kind, then, would not be a deficient or anxious personality but an especially terrifying attack at an emotionally vulnerable time, one that left us wary for years afterward, unconsciously on the lookout for the first signs of its return.

Who knows how far afield we scan for such danger signs? For as soon as we start thinking in these terms, we realize that there is a sort of metaphor-bridge that spans from the physical experience to the purely mental or emotional experience with the result that neither can possibly exist without the other. Being trapped in an elevator has virtually nothing in common with the physical symptoms of an asthma attack, yet the fact that we asthmatics instinctively talk of our experience in terms of claustrophobia, and the claustrophobe talks of feeling as if he can't breathe, suggests that we *feel* (the very word has both meanings) *in both dimensions*. In my phone conversations with my ex-wife I felt trapped, helpless, unable to speak my mind, forced to hold my breath in the hope that the threat would go away. Is it too fanciful to suggest that in doing so I was creating an inner landscape that was all too reminiscent of asthma, setting off my own alarm system?

If one trigger for asthma is in fact an array of sensations that echo asthma, it would explain why a circumstance that provokes asthma in one asthmatic leaves the next unaffected. It doesn't explain *how* fear of asthma triggers asthma, but that's not especially farfetched: the mind-body researchers seem fairly unanimous that nothing is more likely to engender a whole range of physical ailments than feeling frightened and helpless. To speculate a step further, it goes along with the fact that, among "negative" emotions, anxiety and depression are far more often linked with asthma than, say, anger: the first involves helplessness and a holding of breath; the second, a powerful raging, a vigorous exchange of breath.

And though the mechanism of fear is probably neurological, and it may well be impulses along the vagus nerve that cause muscles to contract or mast cells to degranulate, we certainly have the ability to affect our own breathing far more directly, by apparently retraining our muscles. Women in particular can suffer from a condition known as Paradoxical Vocal Cord Dysfunction (PVCD). The vocal cords are muscle groups on each side of the windpipe that usually half-close the windpipe when they are relaxed and open it when they contract. PVCD occurs when, usually after prolonged tension and anxiety, the muscles apparently are somehow instructed to work in reverse, so that when they contract, instead of opening the windpipe, they close it. The harder the sufferer struggles to breathe, the less air she gets. The treatment is exactly what you would expect: drugs to relax the muscles, then psychotherapy to address the causes of the anxiety, then speech therapy to retrain the muscles. Amazingly, I've never run across the suggestion that a similar mechanism may be at work in some forms of asthma (unless one includes Paul Sorvino's intimation of a "mistaken breathing pattern"), even though the entire airway system is enclosed in muscle; the vocal cords are simply a slightly more specialized group of muscles at the head of the airways.

So much for the individual attack triggered by an emotional or emotional-physical experience. It strikes me, though, that a second form of asthma-with-an-emotional-component is all too possible, one that is more chronic than topical. During a three-month period when I was conceiving, designing, and launching a new magazine for the local public radio station I found myself dry-wheezing almost all of the time, sometimes not until evening, sometimes (especially during the magazine launch, when the pressure was at work rather than at home) as early as mid-morning.

Although I felt under pressure (work pressure, air pressure, water pressure, depression, repression, expression—the metaphors dance around each other), this chronic slight wheeze was less like an attack than the phone-call incidents were. It was more constant, more indigenous, and as such reminds me more of the strange lump in the throat and the tension in the arm that apparently took over after my asthma receded.

To me this suggests that asthma can be a habitual disease pathway, one of the many instances in which *a physical susceptibility is used as a means of expressing a general overload to the system.* Some people get headaches, some get flu-like symptoms, some get indigestion—and, as I've suggested earlier, if we knock these down by suppressing the symptoms, who knows what more serious ailment may come along to try to get our attention? If the general overload lasts more than a few weeks, it's as if a groove is worn through our immunity, and the physical condition—the "presenting problem," the doctors call it—appears more readily, more severely. It is not, after all, "merely" psychosomatic, a form of mirage: it is a genuine illness, even if it is also an expression of some more fundamental disturbance to the system.

Asthma, I believe, can be emotionally triggered but also emotionally *maintained;* and is it too much to believe that a constant state of tension, expressed through my particular vulnerability by a steady irritation of the vagus nerve, could contribute to the chronic, never-healing inflammation that is now seen as the cellular fingerprint of asthma?

My final suggestion is the most heretical. Emotions may trigger an asthma attack, my allergist said irritably, but they can't *cause* asthma. Yet I wonder. It's just too much of a coincidence that both my first asthma attack and my first aspirin-sensitive asthma attack took place when I was almost overwhelmed by overwork and by my own particular albatross, my overdeveloped sense of responsibility. This connection seems so strong that I wonder if such intense emotional pressure plays a part not only in triggering some asthma attacks, but, in some people, in *the creation of an allergic response.*

In some cases of asthma, yes, symptoms creep up on us over months, even years, as we develop an increasing sensitivity to an allergen; but in other cases it is as sudden as a dam breaking, and instinct and experience tell me that emotional overload can be such a burden on the body that almost any physical breakdown can result. The circumstances of my November 1991 attack—overwork and a sense of responsibility and helplessness—were so similar to these other two "initiating" attacks that I've wondered if it wasn't a sign of a new allergy, its arrival all the more explosive for being born of such pressure.

I can't tell; but the more I read about allergies, the more they seem to be rogue entities rather than predictable genetic fallibilities. They seem to run in families, certainly, and in many instances their appearance seems to be linked to the degree of exposure to allergens, but the timing of their arrival doesn't follow neat equations, and they also seem to be born of insults to the system—the mother smoking during pregnancy or during the child's infancy, for example. Severe emotional distress is an insult to the system; it seems perfectly possible that it might catapult an allergy from latency into full-blooded existence.

In the end, though, even if the usual extrinsic suspects are to blame for triggering an individual attack (sorry: episode), *the result is nevertheless a psychobiological event.* In the first spring after Barbara and I had met, we spent the weekend at her brother's house in rural New York. The place had been empty all winter, and we went down as caretakers to sweep up dust, mouse turds, and the corpses of a hundred thousand sill-flies, and open the place up for the summer. We decided to sleep outside in a tent, which seemed romantic; but the closer we came to settling down for the night, the tenser and more uneasy I felt. My heart sank: I seemed to be avoiding intimacy, withdrawing into myself—the old warning signs that I was trapped in a bad relationship and was dreading the consequences. I couldn't even bring myself to lie down next to her but stayed propped up on one elbow. *Don't tell me this one's going wrong, too*—but then I caught the echo of my breathing in the hollow of my shoulder and discovered to my surprise that I was asthmatic. This, too, could have been a sign of anxiety, another switch in the cause-and-effect shell game; but luckily I made the opposite assumption, exclaimed, "Good grief! I'm wheezing!" and reached for the albuterol inhaler, thinking, *Of course.* The house was incredibly dusty, the air was full of pollen. How could I have been so stupid? A minute later I could lie down and hold her, feeling several shades of relief.

What do I mean by a psychobiological event? Asthma is an external demonstration of a series of internal events, some of which involve or are influenced by the way in which we understand and deal with the world. (The same is probably true, to perhaps a lesser degree, of most, if not all, illnesses.) But illness is a complex and malleable geometry, in which all the pieces are flexible, and are influenced by and influence each other. An asthma attack, or episode, doesn't present us with only physical symptoms; the attack also creates (and recalls) strong emotions, which are a kind of feedback to the mind in the same way that physical sensations are an information feedback that produces a less consciously considered response. The mind, then, can't help getting involved, and in doing so it creates *meanings,* which may be wildly inaccurate. Such meanings, of which we may be only dimly aware, affect how we interpret the experience and how we will respond to it in the future; they affect how we treat ourselves and what efforts we make to stay healthy in the future. They may even in themselves provoke physical symptoms, and the loop starts again, only with another twist in it.

The way we see the world, then, and the way we see asthma may both be active ingredients in the progress of the illness, for better or worse. In this sense, medicine is really a pursuit of meaning, and the stubborn flourishing of asthma is in part due to the fact that we asthmatics don't know what the hell to make of it, and in many cases the medical profession can't help us much.

Here's a last, perfectly equivocal, example. The worst asthma I had before the age of thirty took place in June 1974, during my final university exams, which at Oxford cover the work not just of a semester but of the previous three years. I had eight three-hour essay exams in five days: two on Thursday, two on Friday, one on Saturday, two on Monday, and one on Tuesday. Late Saturday night I began wheezing and found that I had no Franol tablets. I spent the whole night in an armchair, hunched over, trying to breathe.

It's worth noting that, as with my first attack, it took place before a test, and that as I wheezed away the night, once again I hoped—and assumed—that as I was in such bad shape I wouldn't have to take the exam. (A vain hope: the college doctor introduced me to my first beta-agonist inhaler, my breathing returned to normal in an incredible thirty seconds, and I took the exam shaking so hard I literally had to coordinate my writing to the up-and-down tremor of my hand.)

But, as with my first attack, allergies may have played an important part. It was June, when my seasonal allergies typically kick in—but they hadn't yet appeared, which was why I hadn't yet picked up a supply of Franol tablets. Was it coincidence that the allergy season began in the middle of finals? Or did the attack have nothing to do with allergies? I simply couldn't tell.

What meaning did I derive from this experience? Almost none. At the time, my immediate concern was to stay awake, try to dredge up several thousand words that more or less made sense, then drink a lot of cheap champagne. I learned nothing about asthma; I learned nothing about myself. The only meaning I derived was that I should immediately stop taking Franol tablets and switch to bronchodilating inhalers, which I used for the next twenty years while my asthma got steadily worse.

Oddly enough, even after this cadenza of speculation, I find myself coming back to Aaron Lask. I'm skeptical of his argument that some asthmas spring from—and mask—personality disturbances, but to my own surprise, I want to see the psychiatrists and psychologists, our old antagonists, getting involved in clinical asthma and research again. They've been in the penalty box long enough; we need them out on the ice along with everyone else.

If nothing else, the psychiatrists are likely to ask questions about asthma, or illness in general, as a human experience—a perspective that at the moment is sorely missing. "Who is suffering? The asthmatic or his environment?" Lask asks. It's a stunning question, especially as the word *environment* might refer to our air, or to our family, or to the broad social environment that we call society, and charge with maintaining our health. "And what precisely is the nature of his suffering?" continues Lask. Most important, he realizes that the emotional value of any illness is a crucial and often-ignored component. He continues: "The reticulation of emotions, experiences, events—and their timing—that becomes the asthmatic pathway is of such complexity that it is impossible to separate cause and effect when the asthma finally appears." Lask was writing three decades ago, but *it is still true in 1994, even when we include under "experience and events" all the ingredients—chronic inflammation, vagal stimulation, leukotriene activity—that Lask did not know about.*

All physical sickness has its mental dimension—loss of perspective, mood swings—and while the researchers are discovering more and more physical causes for mental illness, pinning down the defective gene, naming the guilty neurotransmitter, I wonder if we shouldn't also be trying harder to understand the mental dimensions of physical illness. Asthma is more than allergy and inflammation, and someone had better figure out what. Above all, Lask is validating the asthmatic's confusion, the bewildering intertanglement of the inner and outer worlds and of the fields of "pure" medicine and behavior and psychology and pharmacology. *What is the entire experience of asthma?* Lask was asking; and by doing so, he was challenging me, I realized, to take the next steps: What is the entire experience of any illness? Of health? Even—by a simple process of addition—of being alive?

Successfully Ill

O ver the past three decades, asthmatics have been passed around, stolen, bounced about, intercepted, and grabbed for like a basketball; in fact, it's as if half a dozen teams turned up at the local courts with only one ball among them, and they're still haggling over who should play even while the game is in ragged and rowdy progress. The court is full of whirling figures—allergists, hypnotists, psychologists, pulmonologists, neurologists, chiropractors, thoracicists, ENTs, acupuncturists, pediatricians, internists—some making impossibly fancy (and often pointless) moves, others just backing up and calling for a pass. The homeopaths, gentle souls, hardly get to touch the ball at all, while the geneticists, in a neon strip so vivid it scorches the eye, have not even deigned to make their move yet, and are off by themselves doing a series of stretches that nobody else has ever seen. One side says it is up 119–87, the other that the score is tied 44–44, but clearly no end is in sight, and at no foreseeable time will the game be reduced to six players on a side. Only the drug companies, who sponsor the teams and run the refreshment stands, are ahead.

This mad scramble is a sign of several different things: it shows how much money is at stake; it shows that any unexplained disease offers a potentially new and fascinating insight into the body and science in general. It may also show that what we refer to as asthma may actually be not one disease but the symptoms of several diseases: a prenatal elastin deficiency, infantile lung-tissue damage, a classic allergy (though allergies in themselves are probably more complicated than we have been told), tissue disruption caused by an industrial accident, an embedded virus, an autoimmune disorder. Confusingly, any one of these may prepare the ground for one or more of the others or may make the airways one of the body's breaking points at times of emotional crisis.

Asthma may also be changing. All diseases are skirmishes at the borders between order and chaos, between self and non-self, between the past and the future. (What distinguishes disease from other interactions between self and non-self is that disease happens at a level of scale beyond our range of perception; we perceive it by its effects.) If we fight disease in order to maintain self-definition, we are also defined by the struggle: even our victories change us. Conversely, any change in the world will change what happens at our point of intersection with it. Disease will be the unanticipated result of such a change. We are therefore likely to see new diseases or new forms of existing diseases. Through disease, we too will be changed. This will in turn produce new types of encounter, new diseases. Because this new encounter is unanticipated and it also involves change, it is almost bound to be inexplicable in current terms. Because we as humans seem to be exerting more change on the planet than any other force, many—perhaps most—of these changes are ones that we ourselves have brought about. In this sense, disease is one means by which we monitor progress. The most intimate and continuous relationship between our internal world and the world outside is the give-and-take of breathing. One asthmatic may be a sign simply of an unhealthy person; a widespread chronic respiratory illness is a sign of an unhealthy world. Our wheeze is not a complaint but a warning.

As for my own asthma, it seems to have been tethered. These days I catch myself wheezing perhaps once every three months instead of once a day, as I used to. Cold air is no longer a threat; nor is exercise, anxiety, or pollen—though a combination may still push me over the top: my only episode in recent months occurred on a frigid evening at a barn dance where one end of the barn was stacked high with bales of hay and I had had a couple of beers. My airways are simply not as easily or as radically disturbed as they once were. Whenever I get a sore throat I still brace myself for it to slither down and lodge in my airways, to hatch into bronchitis; but I step back up to the full dosage of inhaled steroids, stay warm, avoid talking (as much as possible), and within a day or two it fades away, leaving me astonished, time after time.

On the other hand, I'm tethered, too: I stray only about ten minutes away from my albuterol inhaler and my epinephrine syringe, and about six hours away from my inhaled steroids. If I leave my black washing-tackle-and-pharmaceuticals bag in the car, I'm aware of an invisible elastic band, a radius of safety. For a year or more, whenever I thought about this I got angry all over again, or my heart sank a little. But perhaps this was only novelty. After all, over thirty years I've gotten used to the idea of being tethered to my glasses; the medications are becoming just another of those things—wallet, keys, checkbook, diary—I don't leave home without. On the other hand, inhaled steroids only suppress asthma, they don't cure it; and who knows what the effects of taking them for thirty or forty years will turn out to be?

I'm not worried that I'll get another major attack, and I don't think I'll have one unless I do something stupid, like taking aspirin or ibuprofen—but then that's what I thought two years ago. As far as I can tell, I'm better prepared, but even that may be as much of an illusion of security as the epinephrine turned out to be. All in all, I doubt if I'll ever choose to live more than half an hour away from a hospital.

I worry that Zoë may develop asthma, although so far she seems to have inherited her mother's sensitive skin rather than my sensitive airways.

When I reported my progress to Dave Gannon, a pulmonologist at the University of Vermont College of Medicine, he raised his eyebrows. I was a success story, he said, a walking testimony to inhaled steroids. Later, I wondered, *Why am I in particular a success story?* Why have I done so much better than other asthmatics on this course of treatment? It may be that my asthma was less severe than some people's or that I'm especially in biological sync with inhaled steroids, but I doubt it. I suspect it has more to do with the issues I've been discovering that go beyond my own case and beyond asthma. I suspect it has to do with the entire submerged realm of medicine whose visible tip is called "compliance" and which affects every medical encounter and transaction, and every aspect of our health or illness.

Inhaled steroids, as I discovered at the beginning of this project, are regarded as the state of the medical art, the wonder drug for asthma—at least until a cure is discovered—and they certainly seem to have done me a lot of good. Yet of all the asthmatics I've interviewed, I am one of only two who have consistently followed this course of medication. Some have never been prescribed them, which suggests a dangerous ignorance or conservatism in the medical profession. Many have used them for a while, but as their health has slowly improved they've given them up as the first medication to cut back on, despite their doctor's orders. Some avoid medication and doctors altogether; some use medical care only when they can afford it—or can't avoid it.

At various times in the last two decades I have fallen into every one of these categories; which makes me wonder why I persevered with this extended course of preventive medication now, when I didn't do something similar with cromolyn at the age of thirteen, when it was first prescribed for me, or twenty-eight, when I briefly tried it again. For one thing, I was scared, you may say— but I was actually far more scared in 1984 by my first all-out attack. Inhaled steroids weren't available (at least in the United States, lagging as usual) in 1984—but I very much doubt if I would have stuck with them even if they had been available. No: if I've become a success story it's because I have become *engaged in the process of healing*. This is more than merely taking on a greater responsibility for my own well-being—it's an entirely new way of looking at health, illness, and medicine. In particular, I've realized two things: that all illness presents an opportunity to learn about ourselves and the world we inhabit and create, and that chronic illness in particular challenges us to ask if it is possible to be *successfully ill*.

Illness is a thoroughly confusing state. For a start, we can't trust our own perceptions to tell us what's happening. Our experience of illness is of symptoms; or, to put it the other way around, symptoms are illness as we bring it to our own attention. Our consciousness experiences illness like George III experiencing the American War of Independence: as a series of messages of wildly varying reliability bringing mostly disturbing news from a country he has never seen. And all this while he is receiving hourly reports from every corner of the realm on countless subjects, any of which—fluctuations in the cost of tobacco or tea, an insufficiently deep bow from a foreign ambassador—may be affected by the war, or by a different war, or by something else entirely. And in hearing advice from friends, family, and physicians we are just like poor George, surrounded by courtiers of dubious integrity and advisers of doubtful perspicacity. Who can blame us for going off our rocker, issuing contradictory instructions to the body politic, ordering quick fixes to only the immediate problems, or wanting to let the war wage itself and let us get on with easier problems of government, such as chewing the carpet? (Or was that Hitler?)

And that's only the phenomenology of illness. Illness is also a social, moral, and psychological entity. Those of us who define our value and our identity by what we do, believe we are worthless when circumstances demand that we do nothing except look after ourselves—or, worse still, that we ask others to look after us. We fume, we feel guilty, we despair: work is piling up, the house is messy, we are just being selfish. On top of this, the so-called "wellness movement" has depicted health as a matter of will and of character, so being sick becomes a moral as well as a physical failure, and the more avidly we believe that we should be perfectly healthy, the more illness comes as a nasty surprise, a failure, an insult. Under these mental circumstances, almost anything we are likely to do—drag ourselves into work, take patent medicines to suppress our symptoms, feel resentful and angry—will probably suppress our immune activity and hinder our recovery.

In our frustration and our effort to blame something or someone else for our discomfort and misery, we overlook the fact that illness is not a cause but an activity. By talking of "illness," as in the sentence "She has an illness," we are reifying it—that is, creating an entity that has no independent existence. There is such a thing as suffering, which describes our misery perfectly, and there are symptoms, but there is no such malign entity as illness. Illness is us, working to become healthy.

Just as important as investigating the cellular mechanisms of disease, then, is understanding the experience of illness, to learn, in an unusually literal way, how to make the best of it.

For me, at least, the key was curiosity. It's odd, when you think about it, that someone with an illness has been granted a window into his interior, a chance and an incentive to learn about a whole new world—and yet who ever thinks of it in those terms? What doctor ever begins with "Well, you'll find this interesting . . . ," partly because it is no longer interesting to the doctor, I suppose. And yes, of course being sick is painful and unpleasant, but under the circumstances you'd think that we would want to find anything positive we could from the experience.

This left me wondering, *What can we reasonably expect to gain from illness?* More, surely, than just a return to health. Being an active patient is like fixing one's own car: with each breakdown we learn more about our car, about cars in general; we're less thrown off stride next time, less apprehensive about cars in general. Instead of sending our bodies to the dealer and grumbling about the bill, we discover what goes on under the hood, we love tinkering and tuning, we hear the first sound of the engine running rough early enough to prevent anything serious going wrong, we enjoy the challenge of keeping ourselves running efficiently. We become, perhaps, less apprehensive about life and death, more impressed by our own interior design.

In turn, this has meant that I'm a little more patient with myself as a patient, a little more respectful of the state of being ill, not quite as superstitious and scared as I used to be. What was I thinking when I fell ill, say, ten years ago, when I went to the doctor, when I walked out of his office with my head whirling? All too often, visiting the doctor is like being a seventeen-year-old buying our first used car: we go into it in a thicket of hope, ignorance, and anxiety, hoping to get good, reliable information with which we can make a sensible decision; but once we're on the spot we are told things we barely hear, let alone understand, consider, or remember. By the time it's all over our ambitions have wilted and shrunk, and we'll gladly settle for simply not having acted like a fool.

If this means that in one sense I'm no longer a "good

patient," taking up more than my allotted fifteen minutes, asking too many questions, kicking my doctor's tires, I make no apologies. Almost every aspect of the "doctor-patient encounter" has gradually shifted toward the convenience of the doctor, but I am the one who is ill, and that, too, needs no apology.

In fact, I am in almost every respect a better patient than before, and an increasing amount of medical opinion agrees with my bolshie notion of a "good" patient. The goal of the latest asthma treatment is what is usually called (with the usual medical tin ear for the subtleties of language) "patient empowerment" or "patient education"—in other words, gentling the patient along towards becoming more of her own doctor, monitoring her own symptoms, understanding her own medication, using the physician as a resource. Such a patient may be less grovelingly obedient and indeed may run into conflict with physicians of the older school, but she is also less likely to use medication erratically and irrationally, suffering periodic collapses, alternately avoiding and clinging to the physician, and dashing between the ER and the latest New Age guru. The new model is far cheaper and less demanding on every aspect of our resources: by understanding my condition I assume more and more responsibility for it.

This evolution from the panic-and-superstition patient to the self-aware patient is slow and difficult, and I have little tolerance for a doctor who doesn't understand why. Nothing is as fraught as sickness. Nothing is as laden with embarrassment, fear, anger, resentment, and anxiety. What's more, if the patient faces a long journey toward a kind of enlightenment (not only about a particular illness, but about how to doctor or parent himself best, how to understand himself and make best use of what he has), then the physician, too, has a long and difficult journey from the brittle, shallow certainties of medical school to something more—well, more patient. Nowadays I don't trust young doctors very readily. The physician I respect most is in his early forties, earns no more than I do, and in addition to his rural practice runs a hospice program. He has seen suffering and death and has been altered by them.

We're all altered by illness, in fact, and not necessarily for the worse. Here in the United States we rage against illness—anyone who has been in health care for more than, say, twenty-five years will tell you that Americans have become far more demanding of medicine—insisting that medical science be dispatched like the *Mission: Impossible* team to cure this or stamp out that, just as we are now demanding that our schools fix our trade imbalance and our drug problems. We instinctively believe in our own innocence and perfectibility; we are encouraged to believe that money can buy anything, and that we deserve what we can afford. Illness of any kind, but especially chronic illness, dismays such optimism, defeats such paradigms. *What if it simply can't be helped?* What if the absent asthmatics were right all along, and there is value in learning to make the best of things? It's a common observation, in fact, that children with mild asthma seem to mature more quickly, having learned the adult lesson that we do better to flourish within our limitations. But who ever suggests that illness may be good for us?

(In writing this, I'm suddenly aware that my medical activism and, indeed, this book are a result of coming to the United States, of losing that fatalism, or humility, that sense of limited possibilities that is both the English patient's support and his hindrance. Americans are constantly urged to want; yet medicine, like politics, is the art of the possible. It's a fine balance: to want too little makes us old before our time; to want too much is the germ that breeds bitterness and frustration. In the marketplace, contentment is the first casualty.)

And while illness gets a bum rap in the United States, health is constantly oversold. The American public has long been inspired by improvement and expansion—new prairies to cross, new frontiers to push back, new happiness to pursue, new products to sell, new messages to broadcast. Superior health is one of the latest ideals, perhaps. It's interesting that the most popular health-and-fitness television programs avoid any mention of injury and disease, are set on beaches in paradise, involve an unmistakable element of sexual fantasy, and display expensive exercise wear. Health is a fine thing, but it's all too easily confused with perfection. The notion that health should coexist with illness is a disappointingly cluttered view, a blemished one, one that will never sell. Health is a temporary phenomenon, the flourishing of a state doomed to ultimate collapse; it is bound by history. Health involves the constant death of cells, constant muscle damage and repair. Who knows what would happen, in fact, if a threat-free environment could exist? The constant production, use, and destruction of cells are probably valuable in themselves; like background noise, they may keep the system healthy.

If we're wrong to ask medical science to come up with the physical perfection we've seen advertised on TV then what is medicine's job in this new world of successful illness? I think we can best ask medicine to help us understand ourselves, for if I've learned one thing in the last two years it's this paradox: that although our immune systems work almost entirely independently of our conscious minds, there is no substantial, long-term healing without self-understanding.

Medical science is seen as having two major goals—medical research and clinical treatment of patients—and one minor goal: educating future researchers and clinicians. These branches can all too easily drift apart, leaving more and more medical activities to fall between the cracks, and they can equally easily drift away from the rest of the human world, the research taking place on the lab bench far from the madding, coughing, unpredictable crowd, the clinical work taking place in the doctor's office or the hospital, denying the physician a view of the complex disease dynamics of the home or the workplace.

Medicine needs a pre-specialist goal, a new, unifying sense of purpose to match the emerging understanding of our subtle and complex relationship with illness. Medicine, I think, needs to be seen as a meeting between patient and physician, on equal footing, in the real world, with the aim of promoting self-understanding. With this in mind, we need a new discipline in the medical schools, one that we might call Health Ecology, whose purpose would be to study the relationship between medicine and people. It would have offices in schools and factories and malls; its students would make home stays, not just home visits. It would study not medicine as a science of the body, but *the enactment of medicine* as a human process. It would research behavior and language. It would investigate old medical maxims and myths and find out why they have survived and what their effect is. It would study the way patients listen to doctors, and vice versa; and the way patients speak to doctors, and vice versa. It would investigate what medicine can do, when, and where—a series of questions that in themselves could entirely redefine the role of the doctor, and of the patient.

Above all, Health Ecology assumes that neither the asthmatic nor his environment can ever suffer alone. Disease never involves one cell, nor one organ, nor one tissue—nor one physician, as each doctor is educated by dozens of doctors, reads books and articles written by thousands of doctors based on research conducted with hundreds of thousands of patients and millions of animals involving remedies culled from billions of plants. Likewise, staying healthy involves the activity of hundreds of billions of cells in each person, drawing nourishment from sunlight, air, and organic matter culled from all over the earth, constantly collaborating in the face of an almost-infinite number of threats—many of which we create ourselves, by engaging in warfare, or designing means of transportation that can kill us, or playing professional football. If as individuals, or as a society, or as a species we don't understand ourselves, some of us will always be unhealthy, and all of us will suffer, even (though less obviously) those who prosper and profit from others' disease. Healing is a collective activity, not a commodity—a verb, not a noun. When one person falls ill or stays healthy, the entire universe is involved.

Epilogue

JUNE 9, 1993

At half past midnight I realized I was still awake, my stomach uneasy and my mind racing. It had been a strenuous day. I had decided that, as a fortieth birthday present to myself, I'd take Barbara and Zoë to England to see my family; we were leaving in five days, and I was frantically trying to get the last chapters of this book rewritten before we left. In the morning I discovered that I'd accidentally deleted a short but vital section that I'd written months previously and now had to rewrite from memory. Later, I'd spent two hours frantically turning over everything in the house, from basement to bedroom, looking for a manuscript of a book-in-progress that a physician I barely knew had sent me. What if I had lost it?

As I became more and more tense, the infuriating lump-in-my-throat sensation came back. By now I was convinced that it was actually a cousin of my asthma: with the asthma under control, under stress I now clenched the throat muscles around my esophagus rather than around my trachea. This condition, I had discovered, was called *globus hystericus* and was usually found in women, as "hystericus" implies. Somehow this seemed all of a piece with paradoxical vocal chord dysfunction, which usually affects women under stress, and a weird and otherworldly observation that the psychic had made, that in all the previous times my spirit had visited earth, I had come as a woman, and that this was my first visit as a man—a suggestion that made instant and stunning sense to me, for reasons that will have to wait for my book on the existence of the soul. At any rate, by now such connections no longer seemed especially farfetched, especially in the middle of the night. My stomach felt trapped and bloated, and my mind refused to stop rewriting the chapter on chronic inflammation, so I took a Tums and swung my legs over the side of the bed, hoping that my stomach would feel better if I was more upright. Ever since the attack eighteen months ago, this nocturnal indigestion makes me uneasy. Is it starting all over again? Will the acidity, the turbulence somehow overflow into other systems? Will the anaphylactic reflex kick in? And I wait nervously for the itch in the spine, the crowding, buzzing heat in the ears, mucus pouring out of the goblet cells.

Lightning flashed on the curtains; a storm was moving in from the north.

As I chewed the Tums I found myself thinking, *You know, I never did check to see what was in Rolaids.* I was sure that they wouldn't contain aspirin, but was it possible they'd been in a bottle that had once contained aspirin, or that I'd somehow put aspirin in the Rolaids bottle? Now that I came to think of it, we hadn't thrown away the bottle, which amazed me, given that I had mentally blacklisted them eighteen months previously. Hell, I wasn't sleeping anyway—I got up and walked down the corridor to the bathroom.

The bottle was in a cupboard under the sink. I sat on the toilet seat and looked at the label. Extra Strength Rolaids. Sodium Free. Antacid. Assorted Mint Flavors. Oh, yes, that was right: I had always taken the plain white Rolaids before, but I had bought this larger bottle, containing an assortment of white and green tablets—wintergreen and spearmint, as I recalled—because it had been on sale. I didn't really like wintergreen, and it had struck me at the time that probably other consumers felt the same way, and this assortment was a way of unloading the flavors that weren't selling.

Lightning flashed at the bathroom window. Okay, let's look at the small print. Active ingredient: calcium carbonate 1,000 mg. Also contains: acesulfame potassium, whatever that is, colors (FD&C Blue No. 1, FD&C Yellow No. 5 (Tartrazine) . . .

I don't believe it, I thought. *I don't bloody believe it.*

FD&C Yellow No. 5 (Tartrazine).

I ran downstairs and pulled out Paul & Fafoglia's *All About Asthma*. "Aspirin-sensitive asthmatics have been suspected of being sensitive to tartrazine (a food additive and dye, commonly called FD&C Yellow #5), but this has been by and large overstated. Sensitivity to tartrazine is controversial."

I was so excited I barely slept. Of course, I still had to prove that the Rolaids were the culprit. In the hot flush of my discovery, I lay awake, imagining what I would do. I would take a Seldane to damp down the general reaction, make sure I was up to my dosage of inhaled steroids, go up to the hospital, sit down unannounced in the waiting room outside the ER, take a quarter of a Rolaid, and wait for a reaction. I might have a sign made up already, in case

I couldn't speak: I'M HAVING AN ASTHMA ATTACK BROUGHT ON BY TARTRAZINE. PLEASE TREAT ME AT ONCE. I HAVE HEALTH INSURANCE. As I waited for the effects to kick in, everything would seem to be happening faster and faster, and the excitement would build up like steam. Admittedly, it would be a grandstand play, a little dangerous; I wasn't going to tell Barbara beforehand, and I'd write it up with a warning not to try this kind of thing yourselves, at home. But it was irresistible: I had come this far by myself, and I wanted to finish it off. I even planned the final sentence of my book, a cry of triumph: "The informed patient," I would write, "had done it."

In the morning I called Warner-Lambert, who make Rolaids. The customer-service department representative had never hard of tartrazine, and the medical spec sheet she faxed me made no mention of it. There was no warning that asthmatics should avoid tartrazine, she explained, because Rolaids is an over-the-counter drug, so the FDA doesn't require one. According to the *Dallas Morning News,* in the last quarter of 1992, Warner-Lambert earnings increased 14 percent to a record $1.47 billion. Anxious times are good for makers of antacids.

At the medical library, the American Hospital Formulary Service directory, *AHFS Drug Information 93,* had no doubts or hesitations. Rolaids and Maalox HRF both contained tartrazine, and as far as asthma was concerned, the text explained, "Although the incidence of tartrazine sensitivity is low, it frequently occurs in patients who are sensitive to aspirin."

I nearly went to the ER there and then; but I put it off, and finally came to my senses when Dave Gannon, the pulmonologist, pointed out tactfully that the hospital's Pulmonary Function Lab could carry out a tartrazine challenge for me under supervised circumstances that might avert the possibility of sudden death. Later I realized that this was also my final lesson in becoming the Informed Patient: that one of the most sophisticated levels of patienthood I could attain was to be able to determine when to call in the professionals, and which professional to call; and to go beyond that point was to be merely an anarchic autodidact whose final act was to reject both medical care and common sense. The following morning I went up to the Pulmonary Function Lab. The nurse measured my lung capacity—once again, the largest anyone in the lab had ever seen—and the ease with which I breathed out, which showed the slight obstruction one might expect of a chronic asthmatic. Dave Gannon, who knows a thing or two about an asthmatic's need to bond to a doctor, turned up to make sure everything looked right and hung around to see what happened. Like the others in the lab, he had heard of tartrazine and its potential for asthma, but it had never occurred to him that it might turn up in Rolaids.

I stared at the green antacid on the white counter for a long time. I really, really didn't want to take it. Finally, when I couldn't put it off any longer, I took a quarter of a spearmint tablet—in my mind the more likely culprit, as I didn't like wintergreen and therefore probably hadn't taken one before.

While we waited, Dave and a resident did some checking in the pharmaceutical reference books and the medical computer. In most cases it was impossible to tell what drugs contained what additives: many of them listed simply "coloring." Tartrazine turned up in most of the nonsteroidal anti-inflammatories—after all, Nuprin sells itself on the basis of being yellow. I was sickened: more possible causes of illness were turning up *in medicine itself,* like the poisoned apple. Only the previous day I'd heard from my pharmacist about a girl who, unbeknownst to her mother, was allergic to red dyes. She was fine over the summer vacation, but as soon as she went back to school she became asthmatic, and every time she had an ear infection she began wheezing. The mother herself worked out that her daughter was allergic to the red dye in the Kool-Aid that the school served, and in the amoxicillin that she had been prescribed for the infections. Even prescription drugs are colored to look nice: enormous sums of money are at stake.

For about ten minutes I had the mildest of wheezes, the faint rasp of a snake sliding over sand, but that could have been caused by the normal amount of anxiety involved when you deliberately eat something that might kill you. After twenty minutes I ate another quarter, then another, then half a wintergreen.

After seventy minutes I had to concede that nothing was going to happen. I felt a little deflated. Look, I asked Dave, while I'm here, how about doing an aspirin challenge? Maybe I'm no longer sensitive to aspirin either?

He and his colleague and the nurse glanced at each other, and all of them simultaneously began a verbal encircling maneuver to talk me out of my latest bright idea. Aspirin anaphylaxis, they said, is very, very dangerous; given the option, they'd rather not induce it, even if their lab was specifically set up to deal with pulmonary emergencies. The note of alarm in their voices brought me back to common sense. I thanked them, gathered up my notes, and left.

I was relieved and disappointed; then I realized the whole incident had been one final test, and a rebuke: *How can you still think it could be that simple?* Even after all this time I was still looking for the single causes, simple cures. I still evidently wanted to think that all I had to do was find the one allergen, avoid it, and everything would be fine. I would never have asthma again, and I would live to be a thousand.

Instead, the evidence implicated more complex pathologies: that my attack was brought on by a synergy of several causes, including the debilitating effects of anxiety and the already compromised airways of an asthmatic who has always responded only to his symptoms. Or maybe tartrazine and other factors had indeed caused the attack, but nearly a year and a half of inhaled steroids had stabilized my airways to a point where tartrazine on its own was no longer a threat. That would be extraordinarily good news—for me, and for asthmatics in general.

Nothing had been solved. Asthma remained in many respects as much a mystery as ever. All the same, I was healthier than I had been for years, and as I walked out of the hospital I realized that I was ravenous and curiously elated.

It was time to find some lunch, and then I had a book to finish.

Afterword to the Vintage Edition

In the three years since my major attack in November, 1991, the landscape of my health has changed radically. Although technically I still have asthma, I certainly no longer suffer from it. Maintaining a low dose of inhaled steroids—one puff a day, two or three at the beginning of the pollen season or before I go into a moldy house—is enough to keep my breathing light and easy. I used to use the Ventolin inhaler once or twice a day; I still carry one, but I use it only once or twice a year. I consider myself a recovering asthmatic, to use the fashionable term: I would probably be a fool to take aspirin or ibuprofen, and I'm not sure if I'll ever completely abandon the inhaled steroids, so I'm not cured, but my nightly companion, my echo, my constant wheeze, has vanished. Still more remarkably, I no longer get sinus infections at the slightest irritation to my nasal passages, nor bronchitis after the slightest sore throat. My airways are healthier than they've been since I was ten.

What made the difference? In an immediate sense it was the inhaled steroids, I'm sure, which seem to have stabilized the cellular health of my entire airway system.

("Breathe in through your mouth and out through your nose," my pharmacist said. "That way any medication that hasn't been absorbed in your lungs may help out your sinuses.") Just as importantly, my life is in better order, both at home and at work—less conflict, less self-doubt, less anxiety.

In a broader sense, though, I think I beat asthma (or, more accurately, beat it back) by writing about it. The only way to live successfully with a chronic illness is to become an expert at it, to know so much about it and about yourself that you understand and undertake the best treatments, and know the damp, dark patches in your own behavior that help the illness flourish. Anything less is a well-meaning but doomed combination of superstition and self-deception, and the best medications and the best physicians in the world are helpless against it.

I wish you perseverance and luck in exploring your own asthma, which of course will be different from mine. You may do well with the inhaled steroids as long as you take them faithfully long after you have stopped wheezing; you may do well with less mainstream treatments, though I hope you'll regard them with as much caution as you regard Western medicine. You may even do well on the dried geckos and cockroach gut tea, though if you do, I would like to be the first to hear about it.

TIM BROOKES
January 1995